Angela Fox was born
1912. In 1929 she m
on a theatrical career and in 1935 married
Robin Fox, who became a leading manager and
theatrical agent. She is still deeply involved in the
theatre, and now lives in Cuckfield, Sussex, where
she writes, gardens and entertains her large and
illustrious family.

COMPLETELY FOXED

Angela Fox

FONTANA/Collins

First published by William Collins Sons & Co. Ltd 1989

First issued in Fontana Paperbacks 1990

Copyright © Angela Fox 1989

Printed and bound in Great Britain by
William Collins Sons & Co. Ltd, Glasgow

To David Watson

Contents

Illustrations

Preface

The first volume of my memoirs, *Slightly Foxed*, was published in 1986, and, to my surprise and delight, it seemed to give pleasure. I got such a kick out of it. Suddenly I was communicating with what I am grateful to call a host of new friends. And of course an enemy or two, but that is inevitable. It was gratifying to realize that people identified with my problems, and flattering when I was urged to share some more. So away I went, and this book is the result. If it helps other people who find themselves unexpectedly alone, I may have done something positive, and lightened some bad patches.

Now all the world thinks that their children can be actors – just like that. My own generation, galvanized by my having written a book, assure me that they can do the same. I've given up explaining, because it takes too long and they have no intention of listening, that you do not write a book alone. I owe everything to a team – to Roger Schlesinger, who first saw something I wrote and didn't like it much, but gave me confidence to go on trying because he thought I might Have a Book in Me. He told me I needed an editor and introduced me to Garry O'Connor – such a fine writer and now a very dear friend, without whom *Slightly Foxed* would never have got off the ground.

The person who has suffered most from me is Annie Hirst, whom I rather grandly refer to as My Secretary. She has had an uphill struggle keeping my meanderings in any sort of form and order but always got them off to the right people at the right moment.

Then there was a team of friends at Collins – a little changed now. These days it is Simon King who makes going out to lunch with a publisher the nicest experience anyone can have. Gill Gibbins was my editor before and she, too, became a great friend. This time it is Jane Hill at Collins who has given me such wonderful support. And I am truly lucky that once again Garry O'Connor has worked with me and given me the benefit of the brilliant perception which characterizes his own writing. John Munday, the Collins art director, organized an excellent photo session with brilliant Terry O'Neill that was also great fun thanks to his very special talents.

Finally, I do not write books because my sons are famous and I like to call attention to myself. Through them I get all the attention anyone could need. I write books because, although it may be old-fashioned, I have always found it fun to write to my friends and that is really all I am doing.

Cuckfield,   A.F.
November 1988

PART ONE

1

Stage Struck

Stage struck is what they called me, star struck was nearer the truth. When, to my surprise, I was accepted as a student at the Royal Academy of Dramatic Art, I had no idea of the discipline and regimentation, the conforming to rules, that were deemed necessary to the making of an actress. I had failed at every school except the last one: Avoncliffe in Stratford-on-Avon, 'a school for difficult girls', where I was difficult Angela Worthington.

Avoncliffe was a long, low, white house with a big, wild garden. There was a tennis court which had seen better days, and the pupils would sit in the rockery which sloped down to the Avon and watch the punts glide by, and sometimes boats full of people picnicking and playing the latest hit tunes on their wind-up gramophones – 'If You Knew Susie Like I Knew Susie'. What a heavenly way to spend a summer evening after prep was finished. One day we would enjoy these exciting, sophisticated things for ourselves, but we felt so safe where we were and that we belonged. This is, of course, all that Difficult Girls need.

Doctor and Mrs Box, the school's headmistress, owned the house. He had a very big general practice. They had a son whom we hardly saw and who was preparing to follow in his father's footsteps, and the daughter, Geraldine, was a pupil at the school. She was a very nice girl but, like the rest of the pupils, a bit complicated, and I have an idea that this was the reason for the whole exercise. Mrs Box must have had great energy. She ran the place extremely well and she also had a gift shop in the main street at Stratford.

At Avoncliffe I met someone who wanted to teach me, who thought the task worth while. Someone who taught me to read quite seriously, mostly the essays of Hazlitt and the plays of Shakespeare, particularly *Hamlet*, and who took me and her other Difficult Girls to pretty well every Shakespearian production that was ever performed at Stratford during my two years at the school. For the first time I came under the influence of that rarest of creatures, a real teacher, someone who makes learning a joy. After the theatre we were not even sent straight to bed when we got back, but would sit in her study for hours discussing these plays and the many different ways that they could be interpreted.

Her name was Miss Millicent MacTaggart. How Miss MacTaggart came into their lives I shall never know. She was the retired headmistress of Bromley Old Palace School, where my half-sister, Frances Donaldson, had been a star pupil. Leslie, her mother, must have told my mother about Miss MacTaggart and so it was through her that I came under the guidance of the woman who altered my whole life, by telling me that I was intelligent, and that we would enjoy working together. She set me free. Through her I became an ordinary girl who could do perfectly well if she wished.

Above all, through her I learned to laugh at myself. She gave me confidence.

The classrooms and small dormitories were at the top of the house, but there was a playroom downstairs, and when work was finished there would be marvellous meals like pilchards and cocoa. Miss MacTaggart never complained of the noise and high spirits and the dancing and the singing to the gramophone on the ground floor which went on until the dizzy hour of about nine o'clock.

Mrs Box lived on the ground floor and she had a beautiful drawing-room. The only way to get there was through a personal invitation from her and we knew that we had to take our best side with us. She was a rather fat lady, acting, I feel, the good-natured and tolerant queen bee. Underneath she was observant and shrewd, and it was she who told me, when watching our dancing class while I was struggling to master the fox trot, that I would never make a dancer. She was so right. And, more importantly, she said that I would have many disappointments if I did not learn early in life to give up my fantasy that all my geese were really swans – right again.

Very soon at RADA I sensed that the principal, Sir Kenneth Barnes, whom I never met, regretted accepting me as a pupil as much as I regretted being there, particularly as my mother, who had nobly supported my efforts, had no idea where the money for the fees was coming from. I cannot remember a single class that I got to on time – or even paying attention to a word that was said.

I sat in the common room, mostly eating Cadbury's milk chocolate and biscuits, and giggling a great deal and telling many lies about famous stars that I had met. The other students failed to detect that I was not telling the truth, or at least exaggerating, so I used to get quite a good audience. I was, in fact, watching . . . watching my fellow students all the time. I felt I was a misfit and wished I could escape and have a go at doing something for myself.

I spent days drifting round theatrical agencies, determined to find a job and go out on tour. There were so many of us young hopefuls crammed into tiny waiting-rooms, or sitting on the stairs outside. We got on pretty well together because we shared some dreams, and lots of hopes. Worried, harassed, hungry quite often, and aimless once the agency's doors had shut for the night; what to do with the evening? I did not always want to drift back to the boarding house on Primrose Hill where my mother had found me a room.

It was around that time that some other would-be actor or actress must have taken me to a basement in Baker Street, where the jolliest of Jewish ladies, and one who really knew about the theatre, called Flossie Friedman, made a haven for us all because she understood our dreams. She knew at a glance what we might or might not make of them.

Among the young hopefuls Flossie befriended was an extremely beautiful young woman who at that time called herself Estelle Thompson. She was very, very young, and she later became Merle Oberon, a wife of Alexander Korda and one of the best-known film stars ever. Books have been written about her and she is never referred to as Estelle Thompson, but that was indeed her name, or anyway one that she used. She was a sweet, exquisite, unspoiled Eurasian beauty – affectionate and ready to laugh – and just as broke when we were friends as I was – and that was broke indeed! I never heard her grumble.

I cannot remember giving Flossie money – anyway, I did not have any. It seems that a pupil who could dance taught dancing; I had a go at tap dancing and can remember being absolutely hopeless, but I have never made an audience laugh as much since.

With relief I gave up at once and turned to a young man who played the piano most charmingly, often little numbers he had composed himself, and he would sing, watchful and observant at all times. He would suggest that I sang a little too, and I was pretty hopeless at that, but I liked the way he played the piano so I sat quietly and listened. We became friends. We were the same age, very young and rather wise for our years. His name was Anthony Pelissier.

Anthony was the son of Harry Pelissier, a great comedian of the previous generation. His mother was the beautiful actress Fay Compton, and he was a nephew of Compton Mackenzie, who must have had a big influence on him as he lived with him a great deal when he was a child. It must have been Anthony who took me to see his mother, then starring in a play by Dodie Smith called *Autumn Crocus*. The audience found themselves in the Austrian Tyrol where an uptight, emotionally repressed schoolteacher on holiday was awakened to Love, Life and Passion, for a moment becoming a flower-like beauty due to the attention of a dazzling Tyrolean heart-throb.

I can remember as if it was yesterday the plain, repressed little English woman, played by Fay, in his presence, suddenly snatching a dreadful hat from her head and throwing her glasses to the ground: a radiant beauty, who, with flaming red hair, came alive through love. A passionate – for those days – love scene followed, after which this beautiful creature faded away, as does the Autumn Crocus, and as the Sun Goes Down. All very typical of the theatre then, escapist stuff of course, but sustained by the beauty and magic of Fay Compton.

The heart-throb was played by an Austrian actor, called Franz ('Francis') Lederer. Whether he could act or not, I do not know; I rather doubt it. He did appear later in one other play in the West End and he then seemed to vanish from our lives, but not from mine. I fell in love, and what was so nice was that I did not have to do a thing about it! He was living happily with a lovely girl called Stephie Duna, who was dancing in a Cochran Review at the London Pavilion. He was used to the endless adoration of adolescent girls for he was a matinée idol, and on occasions when I found myself taken to his dressing-room I would just sit and gaze at him. He was kind, because I must have seemed pretty ridiculous: I used to plaster thick white make-up all over my face, ending up with black eyes and a crimson mouth. As I was no beauty, this was not the wisest move, but he was strangely understanding and, one day, as I sat staring at him as he was removing his make-up, he turned to face me and asked, 'What do you really want of life?'

Taken aback by this sudden, direct question, I replied, 'Oh, not to feel like I do now, a mess, not belonging anywhere.'

'Do you want to be an actress?'

'I'm not sure that I ever will be. I'm at RADA learning to act, but this may be only because I want to live in and near theatres, and I want to watch people like Miss Compton and you. I am not sure that I have the courage to do it myself, or even that I really want to.'

Then disaster – I burst into tears. I had told a stranger the truth, and the clown's make-up went for six.

He handed me a cloth and said, 'Wipe all that stuff off,' and he looked at the plain, distraught girl in front of him very kindly, and stretched out a hand for a postcard with his picture on it. He wrote, 'Be what you are in reality and you will be a success,' and he signed it Franz Lederer. I have kept his picture with me all my life. I do not know what his name really was, and I never saw him again. He gave me confidence and, through him, I have simply had a go at whatever turns up. But he did not kill my love of the theatre. I was – I am – stage struck, have always lived in the theatre and with people working in it.

I have never been in love with an actor, nor has one ever loved me, but I have often been in love with their work. This is very fortunate, because it means that I have formed real friendships with men and women whom I not only admire, but to whom I feel gratitude for what they have brought me through their talent; and not just to me, but to thousands, and now – through films and television – even to millions of people. Their faults never matter because, of course, they are more than human, larger than life more often than not, so that the dedication and discipline that they bring to their calling wipes out all critical thoughts.

What I really started to learn during that gust of self-pity in Franz Lederer's dressing-room was that talent is a gift an actor may be born with, but it is the driving, egomaniacal energy, the determination of the person to discard every-thing, very often other human beings as well, for a single-minded obsession that makes a great actor give millions of people pleasure – and, very often, the person nearest to them misery . . . There is also, perish the thought, boredom – resigned boredom if their partners stay the course.

I had a little of the talent, but none of the powers of concentration and fanatical dedication.

I have found that my relationships with the friends that I now cherish in the theatre have, in nearly every instance, started in quite a simple way, sometimes becoming packed with dramas, even difficulties, but always involving laughter. Now that I am much older, these circles seem to have become complete. For example: Anthony Pelissier, who was responsible for helping an impressionable girl to grow up, disappeared from my life for twenty years. Then he came back to play a very important part. My son Edward married his daughter, Tracey, which was most unexpected – and even stranger, Anthony and I shared a grandchild. Immediately prior to his death he learned that we also shared a great-grandchild.

Rex Harrison I first knew when we were penniless unknowns touring the provinces. He had taken up with a girl who had a leading part in a play I was in. I would not have invested in him either. What an idiot! I had not yet learned about actors' determination and dedication, the genius – and I mean genius – of their power of concentration and the application they bring to everything they do. If you do not possess these gifts, then give up, do not try. I was never in their league.

In March 1988 we all went to Rex's eightieth birthday party where he was a host in fine form, remarkable as he was only just recovering from an operation on his eye to remove a cataract. Shortly before that I had been with him and my sister Frances Donaldson and her husband to see a play of our father's, *Canaries Sometimes Sing*, a marvellous comedy, but it failed for various reasons. Rex had just enjoyed a huge success at the Haymarket Theatre in another Lonsdale play that was not really as good, called *Aren't We All?* He did it for a limited season: there was never a seat to be had.

After the theatre Rex took us all to supper at the Ritz – he always lives at the Ritz when he is in London. There was no head-waiter on duty when he arrived, and the under-waiters had not a clue who he was. He never told them, but just fumbled his way from force of habit to the best corner table. He could not read the wine list because he could not see it and so he asked my help and then, until very late at night, held us spellbound, and without saying an unkind word about those involved, explained how *Canaries Sometimes Sing* should have been acted and directed. Lonsdale, he said, knew how to write for actors, and planted in his text numerous technical opportunities for comic exploitation. Such acting, said Rex, is the highest form of challenge one can meet. This present production approached the play superficially and would fail, he predicted – as it did. Had he been in it, it would have been running as I write.

But what really puzzled and pleased him was that some time before we were about to leave the Ritz he had a sudden desire for an unseasonable fruit – raspberries – and every young waiter in the room was at our table trying to please him, wanting to serve him. I still do not think they knew who he was, but at the very end of the meal he signed the bill, and, if he gave them a large tip, I did not see him do it. But, at eighty, pretty well blind, he has charisma – magic. He had a borrowed Rolls-Royce – and he had raspberries!

2

Flight

Since the day I discovered I was the natural daughter of my beautiful mother, Glitters Worthington, and of the world-famous playwright Frederick Lonsdale, laughter has been my defence, the weapon I have used to stave off difficulties. But laughter came from seeing through the pretences of others, seeing other people, as it were, undisguised. After all, every successful play of Freddie's was about people we knew undisguised, and so were the situations they found themselves in. He saw people and their hypocrisies about themselves as funny. He was not very cruel but he was amused; and, of course, he did change the names, which was kinder than I have been.

I remember as a child the huge amusement Freddie and my mother had with one of his most successful comedies, which was about Sir Charles Gill, a well-known judge who had a seaside house in our village. He was a brainy, pompous, very well-known figure of the day. I remember all this vividly so I conclude that it is pretty nigh impossible for a grown-up to fool a child. This distinguished judge, this figure of the law, a household name, in fact, had caused great problems for his daughter in her marriage by his priggish and pompous attitude and his inability, or maybe his refusal, to see the plight that she was in. By the amusing if rather cynical way this was presented, the problem was resolved and the play was a great success – so many of the audience could identify themselves and their problems in it, and still can today.

The reason for Freddie's and Glitters' laughter with their friends – which I can hear to this day – was that Freddie invited the noble judge to join him in his box for the first night. Sir Charles Gill never recognized the totally true picture of himself, and remarked what a splendid, amusing show it was. 'So true to life, you know, there actually are chaps like that!'

Glitters would go and sit with the Lonsdales in their box at first nights of Freddie's plays. The fact that Leslie, his wife, was her hostess, and she was the pretty woman who was the mother of three of his children, may seem strange ... but what was even stranger to most people who hear their story is the fact that, although Freddie's feelings for Glitters faded, Leslie's never did. Her affection for Glitters was real and the mutual friendship was only ended by death. The interest she showed in me, the affection that she gave me, were the most important influences in the growing-up period of my life. I am always hoping that I can bring a bit of the tolerance and amused affection that she showed me into my relationship with my grandchildren and their friends. I also remember that there was a limit, which was healthy, to what she would put up with and I would get spoken to very sharply if I was ever insolent or inconsiderate to my mother. She once told me that, in her opinion, there was nothing in me to match my mother's character and courage.

But the boot was often on the other foot. When Glitters, a most attractive woman – whom I wanted to love, and whom I so wished could at least be pleased with me – was under great stress, she would leave me in no doubt that I was the cause of her troubles, and so I always felt slightly guilty and a nuisance. Life in these early stages was lived in the nursery with Nanny, who assured me that I was 'no oil painting'. She was so right. I was pretty bad news all round, but there I was, and what were they going to do with me? No one seemed to cotton on to the fact that I longed to be liked, and would go to any lengths for this, and make every effort. I knew for certain that nobody would ever love me, but I could get the attention I longed for and wriggle out of the many difficulties I had often created for myself by making the grown-ups laugh.

*

Nothing much has changed. I have tried with all my might and main never to take anything and, above all, anyone, too seriously. I was afraid that some situation would arise that would destroy my defences, and that I would not be up to the weight. This of course is exactly what did happen when Robin Fox, the impresario and theatrical agent, my husband – the clever one, the strong one, the one person despite all our difficulties I had not failed – vanished from life in 1971. I wished I could escape, too, from a life that in fact I had not really found all that amusing, but this was not to be.

I can hear over the years our much-loved family doctor,

Cocky Farr, saying, 'Try growing up.' I can feel deeply for others who lose – not necessarily because of death – a partner. Whatever causes this loss, it is the sense of bereavement that is so hard to contend with.

I understand, too, what is meant by being 'thrown in at the deep end'. I had no idea how to swim to shore, although for so many years I had floundered about in the shallows without actually drowning. No doubt in all marriages there is a great deal of grumbling, but there are so many habits that become like an armour and are taken for granted. Suddenly there is nothing, but nothing.

The first lesson I learned (I had heard it often before, but not bothered to take it in) was, 'You cannot stand still.' I was firmly determined to follow this, so I proceeded with reckless abandon to make every mistake in the book. I am now very, very glad that this was so. Once again I am laughing quite often, and have learned, not too cynically I trust, the wisdom of 'casting one's bread upon the waters'. I am getting nearer to not giving a damn whether people like me or not. Yet I have found that quite often I like some people very much and feel brave enough to admit I need them, and extremely grateful when they need me. This sounds simple; it is not. It took me a long time. First I tried running away, at which I became expert, and it was very expensive and full of surprises, not all of them nice ones.

My first mistake was to think that I could go back to the previous time when I had run away from Robin. I went into my American fantasy, assuring myself that it was the only country where I had ever been happy on my own and that I must return and visit my friend Ronda Keane, Howard Jay Gould's daughter, who was by then married to Carl

Muschenheim, the chest specialist, both of whom I had last seen in 1949.

'Never look back,' advised well-wishers. It became like the reprise of a chorus in a musical. When I was alone at night, nearly always in tears of grief, guilt, and, I have to admit, self-pity, 'Never look back, never look back,' thumped on and on until it was time to get up and I, of course, was ready to go to sleep.

When Robin died I felt that I had been pushed out into a dark, damp, empty street. I could almost hear a huge key in the door locking me out for ever. All I could do was lean against it in despair, because I could hear the noise, in my head, I suppose, of life and of laughter going on inside . . . and it all sounded pretty silly, although I had actually thought it important.

'Never look back' – well, I had to look somewhere. There was today to be coped with. The tempo of life nowadays is so fast there is no time for grief. Doctors look wise, use that overworked word 'stress': 'Now you are suffering from stress, and I think these pills will help, they are the very latest thing on the market.' Their pills will dull an absolutely natural and necessary emotion that nature will cure, given time. I took the pills and entered into my merry widow performance, and set off for America, to Ronda. On my previous visit, for a brief spell, I had enjoyed an escape from a life I was hating and had had a brief glimpse of what I would like to do, to be, if I could be left to myself for a moment. This time the only thing that remained the same was Ronda's generosity.

On my previous visit she and I had been on our own, free – free to dream of what we thought we would do, no ties, no responsibilities. We came and went as we pleased in beautiful Bucks County, Pennsylvania, and at the splendid apartment she took for me on East 54th Street, New York. But now she was a responsible married woman, her husband was *the* Carl Muschenheim, many years her senior, and they had a son, who is himself now a distinguished man. At that time he was an horrific, adolescent, bearded monster, living at home and, as far as I could judge, wishing his parents and their middle-aged, grief-stricken friend would 'get the hell out of his light'. I understood exactly how he felt.

The aeroplane was a little late landing in Boston, but reliable Ronda was there to greet me with warmth and affection, and said we must rush or we would miss the last boat leaving for Martha's Vineyard where she and Carl had bought a holiday home. We flung ourselves and my luggage on board, just as the boat was moving. The sea was dark and dreary, and as the boat throbbed its way through the water, I recalled some lessons I had had at school, given by an eccentric mistress who thought girls must learn mythology. I decided this was the River Styx of the 1970s and I was crossing it.

The Muschenheims had carefully weighed the position of the rather nice house they had bought so that it would keep them as far away from other millionaire escapers as possible. They had a private beach that was not very attractive, and there was never a soul to be seen. But it was just right for Carl and Ronda, who were dedicated bird-watchers. There was a garden, but, like most seaside gardens where the owners do the work – but are never there to do it – it looked pretty barren.

Anxious to pull my weight, to make an effort, to be part of

the holiday scene, I decided to help them in this wilderness. I lighted a bonfire – in times of stress I verge on being what I believe is called a pyromaniac. Ronda and Carl barely ever spoke above a whisper. They were rather like Quakers. I found their soft way of speaking quite nerve-racking, so it came as a relief when they rushed at me and my fire in a dancing frenzy uttering shrieks and yells and hurling cans of water at my jolly blaze. To make a bonfire in America is a crime – already the police were on their way!

'Why?' I asked incredulously.

'Bonfires cause cancer,' they yelled. End of visitor's emotional outlet – Robin had died of cancer. I retired to my bedroom to try to get a grip on myself. I leant my head on the windowpane and thought, 'How silly. It is like going back to childhood. Oh God, get me out of this. I want to go home. If you help me to do this, I will find something to do when I get there. I will stop crying, I promise I will – and I will try to be useful.'

Of course I had realized that the Muschenheims had set out on a holiday which they meant to be really quiet and that they wanted to do absolutely nothing. Carl was an eminent chest specialist with a huge practice in New York, so the efforts they made for me were kindness itself. They took me all over the island. When we went to eat at the Yacht Club, they explained that we were in Edward Kennedy's Chappaquiddick County where a car outing with a girl had ended in tragedy. This had taken place very recently, and I noticed that I could not get the locals whom I met to talk to me about it at all – if the Kennedys were mentioned there would be an awkward silence, and a quick change of subject. Being rather obstinate, my interest was aroused, and I even

walked the course – on a very hot day and while the others
were sailing – that Edward Kennedy was said to have taken
after the tragedy. I then made the biggest *faux pas* of my
visit.

I announced, with very little real knowledge to back it up
(but because I thought by following in his tracks that I had
proved something for myself), that Kennedy was lying. Next
day we were lunching at the Yacht Club, and a grave
Bostonian, who had been introduced as a famous lawyer,
addressed me quietly in the rather grand and snobbish
accent that goes with that city. The gist of what he said
was that if I did not keep my silly, misinformed, English
mouth shut, I would cease to be welcome in paradise, spelt
M-A-R-T-H-A-'S V-I-N-E-Y-A-R-D.

No doubt at all he was right, and more than ever I wanted
to go home, to England, where I was free to say as I pleased.
I would be criticized, but it would be more like, 'Oh shut
up, Angela, you don't know what you are talking about! Now
what *I* think about Edward Kennedy is . . .' and all the group
would join in with views as ill-informed as my own. Then
Edward Kennedy and the conversation concerning him
would be forgotten as quickly as it had started.

I was due to stay a month. After a week I summoned the
courage to say how sorry I was but I knew I must go home.
My hosts feigned polite surprise, continued to be very kind,
and did all they could to persuade me to stay. They thought
out daily treats for me to take my mind off sorrow. We went
to the Atlantic coast. The waves were too huge for my sort
of unathletic English swimming. The car broke down and
got stuck in the sand. I had mislaid my beach shoes and we
had to walk. The sand was so hot that it burnt the soles of

my feet – so I really had crossed the River Styx. And this was Tartarus. It was my hell, anyway, with the sun, the sea, the quiet, and all those millionaires.

For days Carl listened to my vagaries about returning to England. He was patient and kind and gently told me that, with rest and quiet – if I would accept what he said – I would begin to feel more relaxed and be more able to cope. They cared for me like loving friends would look after a spoilt child, but still the desire to leave was too strong. I was determined to go.

One morning I sat down to breakfast with a different Carl, a detached, stern stranger. 'Okay, we understand, go to the telephone. It is over there. You will find the Pan Am number in the book. Go make your reservation.' I was stunned. I could not believe my ears. Someone was telling me to do something for myself. He could not mean it. He did.

I did as I was told, and so made the first effort to stand on my own feet. I made my reservation with Pan Am. I told Carl the day and time of my flight. 'Right,' he said, 'we will take you as far as Boston. We shall leave you at the hotel there because we shall have to take the last boat back.'

They took me. The journey was difficult. Ronda was always a quiet woman, but she was my best and dearest friend, and she spoke not one word to me on the journey. 'What is the matter with her, Carl?'

'You ought to know.'

Good hosts to the end. There was time for me to be driven round and given a short tour of Boston, tea at a hotel, then embarrassed goodbyes, with me ashamed of my ingratitude and of running away, and experiencing the fear I still felt about being alone.

'How shall I get to the airport?'

'Hail a taxi, tell him where you wanna go.' They vanished through the swing doors.

I have never seen Carl again, because very soon after my departure he died. I had hated him at that moment, but see him now as a sensible man, full of understanding and common sense. He knew I would go my own way, make my own mistakes. He set me free to do just that.

3

Sea of Troubles

Now that my sons, Edward, James and Robert, have, since their father died, made names for themselves in the world of entertainment, every acquaintance, on introduction to me, seems to use the same opening sentence, usually getting the names of the sons and what it is they have appeared in mixed up, the refrain being, 'How proud you must be of your boys.' It happens so often that I now assume what has become my 'good mother' look, and reply, 'How kind, how very kind, yes, of course I am.'

But what I actually feel is that to be proud is really not on. 'Pride comes before a fall', etc. If I could look at these sons and their mother through the eyes of a kind stranger, the sensations that would overwhelm me would be amusement and astonishment, because in no way have I ever been the conventional good mother.

I brought them up during a war; their father was a serving officer in the Royal Artillery, fighting mostly in Africa and Italy, and was not a part of their lives from 1939 to 1945. He won the Military Cross and the Polish equivalent of the VC, the *Virtuti Militari*. At the beginning of the war Edward was two and James (who was christened William) was six months old. Having left these shores in 1941, Robin, somewhat mysteriously, did not come home once, even on leave, until he was demobilized in 1945. Looking back, another mystery I cannot solve is how I maintained for the children a comfortable and secure home, however difficult times became.

The kind friends who tell me the pride I ought to feel are also inclined to ask what reasons I would give for three of the same family appearing to be so successful in the world of entertainment. I never manage to find a satisfactory and spontaneous answer, but when I am on my own I do sometimes count our blessings and try to look for an explanation that holds water. Could it be that they always had a place of their own, a nursery to play in, and a very good Nanny who refused to take wages? This was just as well, for there was never any money. The children had routine, discipline and constant love from Nanny Dawson. Of course I loved them too, but old Nanny disapproved of the way I enjoyed myself; perhaps I should feel guilty – I don't. I was spoilt and free to enjoy admiration and parties in a way that very few young women have an opportunity to do today, and I was not bored by my children because of Nanny Dawson. They were her life, she was born with and lived with an understanding of children totally denied to me. We got on famously. War was raging, but we lived simply and in harmony.

This mutual tolerance lasted until the war ended, when Canadian and American friends who had made homes with us and become part of our family packed up, said goodbye and went back to the girls they had married what must have seemed a long time ago. Without conceit I know they left with some regret, just as Robin walked back into our lives with regret for having left the friends and homes that had become his during those years.

Poor Robin, poor me, poor all of us. A stranger walked in and interrupted our routine. He was now, in fact, a bit of a hero, covered in medals, and brave and courageous, loved and respected by all ranks, by officers and soldiers alike, who had joined him in risking their lives time and time again on our behalf. What I saw was not the irresponsible boy I remembered, but a worn-out, rather handsome stranger with whom I was to be immediately linked in the struggle to deal with most basic post-war problems, the struggle to survive at all. Goodbye to fun and laughter and a feeling of irresponsible adventure – or whatever it was you risk when you are free, for, if you so choose in wartime, you can be free. 'You can be your own man', as my grandchildren would say today, as you seldom can when there is peace – so-called. To use another expression of my grandsons, we had to 'get down to the nitty-gritty'.

Robin had grown used to giving orders, but he did not ever again wish to live with too much discipline, he had had enough. Nanny must go, he could not stand her bossy ways. She went. It was a Black Day. Perhaps I have never really grown up. Even now, all these years later, I never want to live that day again. It is linked in my mind with my mother giving *my* nanny the sack on a staircase leading to my own nursery when I was a little girl, because my mother was in a rage and, affected by the pressures she was under at that time, could not bear the woman another minute.

Something very, very good, some very sound values departed with Nanny Dawson in her little brown suitcase tied up with string because it was too full. She took with her something mothers cannot give their children – steady, uncomplicated love. Indeed, I do wonder so often about how much my sons benefited from all she taught them and me, and how much we all owe her and all she stood for.

Her sister was married to a chemist in Bath and they were going to make room for her to stay with them. I kept in touch, of course, but not for long because she died, and the question I always ask myself is, 'Can people die of a broken heart?' I believe they can, and that Nanny Dawson did, because when she left me she said, 'I would have gone in a little while, but it has all come a bit soon. I hadn't quite finished all that I wanted to do for them.'

My own maternal instinct went as far as longing, in my early twenties, for healthy, beautiful babies that I did not have to look after, and they had to be beautiful, or even this instinct would have vanished. I got what I wanted, but if they were tiresome or ill – normal, that is – Nanny took over, sorted out the moods and upsets that irritated me, and restored them to health and beauty.

When she left, I did from the material point of view all the right things, I kept the same home always, and somehow there was warmth and good food, an achievement in those days which no one would understand now. So often I longed to pack my bag and leave, the simple fact being that I was not very good at being a mother, the job bored me, but I loved the boys, and so I chose to stay. It wasn't easy, because their father and I had not met for three years, and we had both changed so much. In our separate ways we had learned about taking on responsibility, and we were very different individuals from the two who had bade each other a sad goodbye in 1941. I have always wondered if we would ever have tried to stay together if it had not been for the children.

Looking back I believe we still would have done so, because we shared the same values. We made mistakes, we behaved badly, mostly to each other, but when Robin died, I lost the friend I had admired more than anyone, and this is still the case. However, in 1945 I had to learn that the years we spent apart had taken with them our youthful, romantic feelings for each other. He was exceedingly attractive to women, and his name in our world was linked with many beautiful people. Of course I minded passionately the pain and trampled vanity, call it jealousy if you like. Did I have the choice? It was either let him go, something he begged me all our lives together not to do; or come to terms, relax, accept him as he was with his sexual and temperamental needs. I never hesitated – he needed me and of course I needed him. It was important to try to be happy, and now was the time to make the effort to put someone else first. There were many things necessary to him: his men friends, particularly Michael Sieff and Robert Morley; and far more important than any woman was his work, which he loved and at which he was uniquely successful. His relaxations were bridge, golf and women – the last always took far more trouble over him than he over them and I got on quite well with most of them. I could never rely on what Robin might do to me, or not do to me, but I always relied on what he thought, how when something really mattered to us, his thinking was balanced, detached, fair.

Life was sometimes pretty violent between Robin and myself, a slanging match, but all that dropped away when it was our sons that we were worried about. I think one more way in which they were lucky was that their parents never had a single disagreement concerning them. What we wanted for them was a secure home and the best education for life that we could and would and did, as we saw it, make possible for them. Where the young ones were concerned, we were always in harmony, and if this has been to their advantage, I will take half the credit. I could be very irritable, difficult, bored and boring, but Robin was always balanced, always keeping on an even keel regarding the children, and he controlled and influenced me. I did do a lot for them and with them, but I consider this to be what mothers are for, and I was always backed up by his common sense, understanding and even compassion when things got difficult for them. He liked his children, accepted that they would, as they did, have problems, and he would help overcome the difficulties of growing up, more often than not, by making them laugh at themselves, teaching them that they had to accept those in authority whilst not always taking them too seriously. Through witnessing us together they learned to look at people, to observe them constantly, to see why they did as they did, were as they were – and perhaps that comes into their work in the theatre.

Certainly I am left with three sons who can be very companionable, with whom I talk a great deal, even if that is mostly on the telephone. Of course they can enrage me and be difficult, but if they stop in their tracks, they can be caring and understanding without being patronizing. All this is very pleasing, but I do not feel proud – just grateful.

*

It was in the summer of 1971 that James first brought Mary Piper to see me in Eaton Square. I had seen so many beautiful, glamorous and famous girls come and go over a number of years, and I had often felt murderous towards strange Sarah Miles, who was the most important among them. I had even come to enjoy her company because she was so nice to me, but I shed many tears because I knew this magnetic creature, who was then still immature, had it in her power to destroy him. She had, as now, an enormous personality and has never engendered lukewarm feelings in anybody. And she is of course a tremendously attractive woman. Anyone who sees the film *The Servant* must be aware that here were two potential stars. They were deeply in love at the time, but their lives have gone very separate ways.

Mary Piper was a nurse – a theatre sister at St Thomas's Hospital at the time, although she and James met in Sheffield. She radiated great calm. I thought her an amiable girl, liked her well enough, realized we had nothing in common and shrugged that off, thinking what does it matter if they are happy together? I still feel that is all that matters.

The most unlikely wedding between my film star son and Mary Piper took place on 12 September 1973, at St Peter's, Southborough, just outside Tunbridge Wells. Despite my reservations, I had gladly made a material contribution to the day by paying Irish Ken Turner to do the flowers. Assisted by Peta Berry, who had greatly influenced him, Ken worked his magic and turned that rather ordinary church into an Aladdin's cave more beautiful than anything seen in pantomime, filled not with jewels but with the most exquisite flowers.

When we were settled in our seats for the ceremony, it was as if two rather bemused, slightly hostile teams had assembled in a church before an important match. The only members in the opposition pews my family or I had ever met were Mary's parents, Alan and Katie Piper. If they were as bemused and harassed as I was by the coming together of this unlikely couple, they have never let on, then or since. They were and still are very nice to me always; we visit each other once or twice a year. Alan's work had taken him to Africa, possibly in mining, but he speaks very little about himself. I did not know his family or anything of his background, but that the bride had spent much of her youth in Africa, I did learn. She attended Nairobi High School and was a brilliant mathematician, but it is impossible to get them to talk about themselves . . . not like the Foxes.

I was luckier than they that day; I was supported by rather a large family and a good many of my closest friends. I have the impression that it was Alan and Katie who were more the loners. They may not have been back in England very long, and so their part of the congregation was made up of very much younger people, as strange to them as they were to us. They may have been very worthy and worth while, but they were very young and referred to themselves as Born Again Christians.

James's side was composed more of my generation than his own. A jolly and rather garrulous group set out from Ockenden Cottage, heralded by Robert Morley. A dear contemporary of mine, a London friend, Betty Eliot, rather rich, Jewish, was another in the group. She seemed to look upon our family as her own and she loved to be in on the game. My son Robert's old nanny, Ruth Belshaw, was with us, and Betty Foster, who ran my London life. So were two young people: Michael Broadhurst, a regular soldier who had met James when the latter was doing his National Service in the Coldstream Guards, and Damian Greenish, who had been at Harrow with Robert. Damian brought me a beautiful bunch of roses that he had obviously picked from a garden – they had never seen a shop. They remain in my memory as a very special kindness and as a symbol of awareness of difficult situations in the young that we do not always give them credit for. Of course Edward was there, togged up in rather immaculate Edward VIII style.

My other son, Robert, made up the party, having joined the long list of Moss Brothers' customers. His hair was very long and he was not – for once – wearing the most dreadful dark-blue velvet jacket that he insisted he liked. I would have liked to have made it possible for him to buy suits in Savile Row but that was not what he wanted at that period. Had I ever been able to dominate him, would he have become the successful and finally happy and real man that he is now? I think I know the answer. I have given up feeling guilty on that score, anyway.

I must not forget that Mary Carter, who worked for me then, and does now, at Cuckfield, brought up the tail. We had a good deal of champagne before we started and Mary had to be called in from the kitchen sink because, of course, she wanted to wash up all the glasses before we set out in high spirits for Tunbridge Wells. We were very nearly late for the off, because we could not go without her and she disappeared to see that all the doors were locked; she was absolutely certain that the house would be ransacked by burglars – if it was not burnt to the ground. Mary is a dear, but every day for her disaster impends.

No birth, death or marriage for forty years had gone unsupervised by the family doctor, Cocky Farr, so he was, as always, keeping a watchful eye on the group. He knew more of how each one of us really felt than we did ourselves.

Cocky died very recently. His death was recorded in *The Times*, which said he was eighty-two, and that is about all. In fact, he had had a much earlier death when the NHS, of which he approved, forced him to resign as a consultant long before it seemed necessary. Bureaucratic rules had denied him the reason to go on living at all and we Foxes and many patients, particularly those needing his vast experience in obstetrics and gynaecology, which was his field, were denied the help of this dedicated doctor. He was a bachelor who chose to work twenty-four hours out of twenty-four all his life. This stopped abruptly in one day. Sadly for him he continued breathing. He became intensely depressed but mustered up courage.

He learned to play bridge; he went to painting classes; he bought an expensive bicycle and toured round the countryside on that, because as despair and loneliness enfolded him, so the good health that he had always enjoyed began to slip away. He had been an above-average car driver, having practical skill and very fast reactions, but his eyesight and his hearing started to dim; so did his interest in the health of others, whom he had observed all his life and selflessly attended in his vast practice. The Fox family felt very lost.

He no longer wanted to know of the aches and pains and stresses and emotional and physical agonies that he had helped us through for forty years. Because he had never married, the Fox boys were almost like sons to him. He was, apparently, an unsophisticated man, but observant and shrewd and, as a diagnostician, sometimes a genius. We owed him so much – at times even our very lives. I will confess I find – perhaps I always will – life very different and sometimes dreadfully difficult without him. I have to say that I depended on his unselfish goodness and wisdom far too much.

He had seen it all. He knew it all.

*

I remember not putting on my wedding hat until I absolutely had to, because, although I still owned a most elegant coat made when Robin and I had been in Paris one time, I had no hat that quite came up to that standard. But I did have a rich friend called Gay Leigh (Mrs Claude Leigh), who led a ceaselessly social life and had a huge wardrobe. 'Can I borrow a hat, Gay?' I had asked her.

'But of course, dear. What colour is your outfit?'

'A brown silk coat Molyneux made for me.'

'Oh you won't like the only hat that will go with that, it is my gardening hat.'

'Let's have a look.' She produced a beautiful brown hat, the label inside said Worth. It was simple, extremely elegant and looked brand new. 'How can this be your gardening hat?'

'Well, it's no good for anything now, dear, I had it made for Ascot . . . last year.' So away I had gone with this fragile creation. I now looked damned silly in it as it had been made most carefully for quite another sort of face.

The church was on a village green at Southborough. It certainly was not very old; it had been built by a rich man who sited it the wrong way round. I thought, cynically, 'That fits.'

As we made for our seats, I got a glimpse of Marcus Sieff, and was most surprised to see Johnny Shannon and his wife, whom James had known in the old days. Johnny had been working at the Thomas à Becket in the Old Kent Road. I remember him as very much part of the group there. He had taken up acting and he was by no means untalented; a very different James Fox from the one we saw on his wedding day had arranged for him to have a part in *Performance*, a most violent and terrifying film that James had not only starred in, but had taken a responsible part in at all levels of its production.

As we sat, I looked at my sons, James – the bridegroom – and Edward, standing near him, as they waited for the bride to arrive. I found it difficult to recognize James as my son, indeed I wondered who he was. By this time he had become identified with the 'Born Again' evangelical group called the Navigators to which he and Mary still belong. He did nothing wrong, I repeat nothing wrong, he had just become a stranger to me. Perhaps he was a better man than the golden boy I remembered. I had been upset when Joe Losey cast him in *The Servant* – when I remonstrated Joe had replied, 'Well, that's the guy he really is, honey' – but I felt even sadder now and more estranged. I wondered why positive Joe had not seen this completely different side of James's character.

The ceremony pursued a conventional course, with Marcus Sieff singing the hymns lustily out of tune – for so many years we had enjoyed a joke about our dear friend's singing. Finally came the item listed as 'The Address'.

Into the pulpit sprang a film-star type of American, even better looking, if that were possible, than Robert Redford. He was immaculately turned out and certainly he had not had to get his morning coat from Moss Bros. Of course the typical American Evangelist was a novel phenomenon to us then, although today they do crop up on our own television screens – the plausible fellows.

He set about telling us with gusto that he was this young couple's closest and most intimate friend. He thanked God a great deal for this during the tirade that followed. He told us that he was going to give us a talk on marriage, and he settled down to do just that. It seemed endless and was acutely embarrassing, full of clichés and bad taste references to his personal experience of 'the marriage situation'.

Perhaps I never had a sense of humour – or it had never been so sorely tried in my life. A real rage that I had no idea was in me took over. I tried inwardly to talk to myself and calm down. 'Pull yourself together. What does it matter? James is well, he is marrying a girl he loves.' And so on. I was lost. I did not understand. I did not know where the beautiful, obstinate child had strayed to. The man the American Evangelist kept referring to was no one I had ever encountered in my life. I remember thinking that I should thank God that death had saved Robin from this occasion. I believe he would have found it even sadder than I did.

I did try to put a good face on it, but my flippant perform-ance took over when I was the mother-in-law who stood in line prior to the wedding breakfast to shake hands with so many total strangers. Let me make it clear, I am not claiming that I behaved well, but I did feel rather that I was the stranger greeting a most unusual and slightly antagonistic tribe.

Edward was not his brother's best man – despite the morning coat hired for the day. The new Navigator was defying family convention, and as the brothers had enjoyed all their lives an unbroken friendship and closeness, I have little doubt that he caused pain. And certainly when Edward was called upon to speak at the wedding breakfast, I cannot imagine why, he said that the way the occasion had turned out made this very difficult for him, and all he could do was to quote Shakespeare's lines from *As You Like It* when Duke Senior outlines the way in which the uses of adversity can be sweet.

It is possible, I suppose, that sometimes we do not wish to remember details in our lives. In fact to get a true picture of the wedding I turned to Mary Carter, whom I always question when I want to remember something as accurately as possible about the family.

'You will remember the best man, Mary – I don't.'

'Yes you do, he was the first Navigator James brought here, and you had to get them to explain whatever Navigator meant. He was a little fair man with a name like Simms or Simmonds. He had a wife and two very quiet children who had to say a very long grace before lunch. They all seemed ever so good and they were so polite to James that you kept laughing and you asked the fair gentleman what he did when he was not Navigating.'

'What did he say?'

'He could not give you a very clear answer, and you were very cross with them after they had gone, and you said you wondered who paid for all this nonsense.'

That last bit I do recall and I still wonder. Anyway, Mary assures me this not too colourful personality was my son's best man.

The venue for the wedding breakfast I recall rather dimly. There was a sort of mock-Tudor feeling to the room, and I know that I felt isolated from the bridegroom, who had now gathered around him a lot of fairly harmless-looking people who were over-impressed by him. I suppose I felt really that they were sycophantic strangers.

Of the bride's guests, just one person stood out, a quiet, distinguished-looking, middle-aged woman in a grey coat and skirt, almost like a uniform, but obviously her going-to-social-occasions outfit. She came to say goodbye to me and her manner was cold and aloof. 'I hope you have enjoyed yourself,' I remarked. Then she let me have it. She told me that she had no reason to admire my apparently cynical attitude to the occasion, which she had been closely observing. Ready to apologize profusely, I said I was sorry but I did not know her name.

'That is of no importance, but Mary has worked for me at St Thomas's Hospital for quite a long period. She was quite one of my finest sisters, and a better young woman you will never meet, or a finer member of her profession.'

And away she went. She was too well-behaved to add, 'Put a sock in that, Angela Fox, with your silly theatrical values.'

She was right about Mary – a better person and a more forgiving one I never will meet. But at last I feel detached

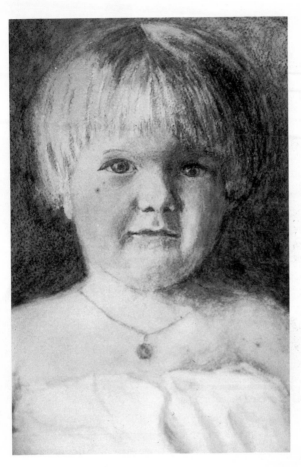

1 My portrait, aged two, 1914

2 Michael Sieff and Robin Fox at Cap-Ferrat, 1966

3 With Jackie Charlton, shooting at Harewood, 1986

4 With Dirk Bogarde and Anthony Forward at Château Neuf de Grasse, 1969

5 With Sir John Clements and Edward, 1980

6 Godfrey Winn and Gladys Cooper in Godfrey's garden, 1964

7 Edward with producer Joe Levine during filming of *A Bridge Too Far*, 1976

enough to say this does not make the Foxes and their loves and interests wrong, though I do wish I understood her world and her way of seeing it better than I do.

The Fox party stayed the course, but, finally, when the last guests were making for home, we piled into our cars. Betty Eliot was at the wheel of the one I got into and she drove us from Kent to Sussex through a crashing, blinding thunderstorm. Selfish as ever, I thought the Navigators really had a line to God who quite clearly saw fit to rebuke me thus. I was oblivious to the fact that there were thousands of other people just in these two counties enduring the same storm who had never heard of the Navigators or the Foxes.

The party that had set out from Ockenden Cottage that morning gathered for a riotous supper party. Two guests were added, Johnny Shannon and his wife. They may have felt that they were as much strangers at the wedding as I was. They had known James only during the period of that violent, decadent and, at times, I admit, brilliant film, *Performance* – what must they have made of the part he had decided to make his own today? A role that he had created and sustained with his acute eye for detail, the same gift he had applied quite brilliantly to such different characters as Tony in *The Servant*, Jimmy Smith in *Thoroughly Modern Millie*, for which he had mastered the art of juggling, amongst other things, and as Marlow in *King Rat*, in my opinion the most harrowing and moving performance he has ever given. He had followed this with one of the carefree, debonair young men in *Those Magnificent Men in Their Flying Machines*. This last character was the one that for many years he had brought home to me. I am his mother, I had believed it was true. You will see that I had some surprises.

Over the last few years I had become rather morose and was always thinking, 'How long is he going to hide what I believe is his God-given talent, and why is he doing it?'

The supper party was fun because there was a sense of relief that a difficult day, full of hidden emotions, was behind us. However, it ended abruptly with tragedy only a fraction of an inch away. It was getting very late, but I asked Michael Broadhurst to open yet another bottle of champagne. He was willing, it could be that he was too willing – as he was extracting the cork it played a trick, and with immense force landed slap in his eye. Yet again thank God for Cocky Farr, who knew the danger at once. Quiet fell upon us as he rang the Brighton Eye Hospital and said it was a serious case. He went to get his car. All we could do was hold Michael's hand; he was in great pain and discomfort, but less surprised than most of us would have been as he had done several periods of service with the Coldstream Guards in Ireland.

So the wedding day finally ended. The Shannons set out for London, the rest of us drifted forlornly to our rooms, not Fox-obsessed any longer, only wondering and caring about what would happen to Michael's sight, even his life. A silly accident had caused a huge injury, and maybe had restored my sense of proportion.

There was, in fact, a happy ending. After quite a long time in hospital, Michael recovered completely and was able to see as well as ever before.

*

In 1988, looking back on James's wedding and his married life, as I do so often, and that agonizingly sad period – sad because I could not make head or tail of what I had done wrong – I feel better now because I do not feel nearly so personally responsible. It is so vain of parents both to feel responsibility for their children's failures and to claim a share in their successes.

What I have loved to see is that he has had fourteen years of a happy marriage. He has five rip-roaring children, and Mary, his wife, whom I did not always understand, and to whom I was unkind and intolerant, was, in fact, the very girl he needed, and a great strength to him. Before he met her I think he felt he had enjoyed too much worldly success far too easily. He had lived in a sort of playboy dream world. He was a very glamorous figure, certainly with star quality. He could rent a house on Malibu Beach or stay in hotels in Paris or Rome or New York if a mood drew him to these places. He had a beautiful house in London, and perhaps he felt that this worldly emptiness had been achieved without either sufficient effort or the best of which he was capable being put into it, and he was seeking truer values; he was not liking himself and the admiration of other people did not seem important.

He was unhappy, and when the Evangelists approached him, he felt he was being offered a way of leading a far more worthwhile life. I know very little about the Navigators and was ever ready to air my ignorance. Now I no longer argue, as I did, or behave aggressively, but I am not so sure that I was wrong about American Evangelists, leaving aside famous men like Billy Graham; the television coverage we get here of their activities makes them look fairly suspect.

James and I used to argue; to be honest, we had blazing rows, even tears. I was obstinate, obtuse, as I would not have been if he had said he wanted to go and study at a theological college, and go into the Church. I suppose I was angry with myself, for the most part, as I had tried to bring him up carefully as the conventional disciplined boy, even to the extent of taking him to Matins on Sundays in his best blue suit. Idiot. That I should think like that was enough. Even now I may be 100 per cent wrong in my understanding – and I shall die trying to understand – but I shall not feel the same ignorant intolerance again.

A lot of this change in James is due to Mary. She and I are totally different in character and temperament. The difficult one was me: sometimes irritable, sometimes laughing. She always showed the same relaxed tolerance. Now we have become very good friends indeed. She puts him and his wishes and his work, now that he has returned to acting, before everything else, and together they have become the parents of interested and motivated children. I could have been termed extremely intolerant of their rather relaxed, undisciplined, easy-going methods as parents – more fool me. The eldest one has just got into Harrow with flying colours, and he and the rest excel at every game. This is in his case a triumph because two years ago he was in Great Ormond Street Hospital undergoing terrifying treatments in an effort to make surgery unnecessary. Finally this was unavoidable. He has recovered completely and is proudly getting up each day to do a paper round near their home before setting out for school. Heaven knows what the future holds, but for all my disapproval I have to laugh at myself because James and Mary's children appear to be hard-working, born leaders.

This is all a pleasant surprise for me because my own

three sons never did a stroke of work at school, played games rather well but only to enjoy them, and rebelled and left Harrow long before they had passed all the necessary exams. They were all mavericks and wanted to do it their way – an attitude, now I come to think of it, that they might just have inherited from me.

4

It Didn't Begin at Home

'Ah, Mrs Fox, you have come to find something to worry about. Do sit down.' The urbane lawyer then pressed a button and spoke into a box. 'Ah, Miss Pilchard, Mrs Fox could do with a cup of tea. She feels a little distressed.' With that understatement, he would then advance into cloud-cuckoo-land. 'I don't see any need to dispense with your charming flat until the estate is finalized. Your executor has agreed to pay the rent. Why shouldn't a woman in your position have a home in Eaton Square?'

My position? My needs? The rascal was dotty. A middle-aged woman on her own, with a lifestyle that had once merited a large flat in the most expensive part of London, had found her resources suddenly cut short. What was he on about?

I did go on with this way of living for a couple more years, helped enormously by someone I met in the street outside the flat, who came up to me and spontaneously expressed her sympathy and asked if there was anything she could do.

'Certainly,' I replied. 'Come and help me keep the white

elephant clean.' This was Betty Foster, and she has been an invaluable help and support ever since then, first to me and now to my son Edward and his family.

Between us we kept the flat looking good, and it was somewhere that Edward and James and Robert could turn up and use if and when they wanted, which they did. They brought many of their young friends with them, and so did me the good turn of starting me on the only road to take, the one that looks forward and not back.

*

Part of this recovery period was spent in a series of 'good works'. Nowadays I am very suspicious of voluntary do-good-ers, because, looking back, I know I should question myself about the many schemes I became involved in. Even at the time I had to laugh at myself and feel guilty if ever I was thanked for my efforts, because my motives were entirely selfish. I was running away and I could always hear my mother's voice saying, 'Get something to do, my girl, justify your existence.' I was trying to turn my back on problems I didn't understand concerning legal and financial matters that seemed to me a lot of gibberish. My efforts, ostensibly to help others who had more problems than I had ever had to face, have, in fact, done me nothing but good. New doors have continually opened and wonderful friends have walked through – ones that have lasted.

The then new Vicar of St Peter's, Eaton Square, the Reverend Desmond Tillyer, was one of these people. It was through him that I took my first nervous step as a small-time do-gooder. We bumped into each other on the pavement in

Eaton Square. I invited him up to the flat to have a drink, but he did not drink, so he had a piece of Betty's fruit cake and a cup of tea.

He was a shrewd, observant young man, and he must have seen at once that Betty and I would fit into a plan that he had, which was to enable people working in offices in the vicinity to attend his church at lunchtime, that being their only hour of respite when they could pray together and be quiet for a while. But this, of course, meant they would get nothing to eat.

Betty and I volunteered immediately to be tea girls twice a week, and down to the crypt we would go and knock up bangers and mash, or quiche lorraine, or whatever took our fancy, and, of course, ice cream and Nescafé. And then, of course, we would wash up and leave the crypt better than we had found it. Up went my spirits; I had found a purpose, a very small one, but a purpose.

Best of all, our stints at the stove, so that others could actually talk to God, were shared by a most charming couple, Mr and Mrs Charles Renton. She was great fun, capable and friendly. He was a quiet man and very elegant. I have said before how my mother judged a man's social standing by the shoes he wore. Mr Renton would have got ten out of ten. I am sure they were made by Lobb, but he stood in them squarely when it was his turn at the sink.

The Rentons asked me for a drink, so it was really they who opened the next door to me, and put in place another small piece of the jigsaw of my new life. In I went. They had a very nice house in a mews near the church. I learned that she was the sister of Rosita Forbes, a noted beauty, traveller and writer in her time. Stranger still, their son was Tim

Renton, the Member of Parliament for whom I voted then and still do.

A second escape route to a sort of sanity was opened when I became a member of the board of the Theatre Upstairs at the Royal Court. St Peter's and the Court were within a quarter of a mile of each other, both in their different ways trying to say something they thought might help us.

*

In one respect, becoming a widow reminded me of the time when I was a young, out-of-work actress who belonged nowhere, to no one. By now the years have taught me that this was a slight invention of my imagination: I thought I was unique. But I knew then that I must always go it alone, not only in a practical way, but, above all, emotionally. Never depend on a man because he would always leave, always let you down. I have stayed liking men very much, partly because I have accepted that they are all like my father. They either leave their women, as he left my mother, because it is in their nature to do that, or they spend a great deal of time wishing they could leave and do not do it because they have not got the guts.

The cruel trick that life plays on women is that they not only like, possibly love, their men, but they actually get to depend on them, think they can lean on them, needing them in so many ways. I donned an armour that I thought, when it was my turn to receive their favours, would make it possible to enjoy everything men had to give, but remain absolutely untouched when they departed to make other acquisitions, as I knew they must. Of course the armour was too fragile, and the arrows of fate struck home with great accuracy, piercing when I thought nothing could get through what I had built up in resistance. I was young, rather attractive, pregnant with Edward.

One evening, I was combing my hair and seeing in the looking-glass a girl and thinking, 'Not bad, not too bad at all.' I rather had the feeling that I had made it, everything was going my way. Robin was lying on the bed, reading *The Times*, relaxing while I got on idly applying face powder, preparing to go out to dinner with him. He put down the paper for just a moment. 'You know I shall never be faithful to you. I shall sleep with whom I like when I like.'

He picked up *The Times*, continued to read and I continued to comb my hair. I acquired at that moment a heavier, even sturdier armour, never very comfortable to wear. Robin was true to his word and it was only when, after thirty-seven years of great friendship together, we were facing his death that I threw away the armour, knowing how idiotic it was of me to have ever believed that it had been of the faintest use.

Like everyone else, I am vulnerable and should have come to terms with that fact long before. We are all stuck with our own natures and whatever agony I am capable of feeling was mine when he finally left, this time for the last time, and he would never come back, as he had done for thirty-seven years.

I think I must be very slow to learn because when he had gone, I hardly knew my name. I had had his name. I was Mrs Robin Fox.

*

I did not waste my time at the Royal Court Theatre as much as I wasted other people's, because I met John Simpson, who later became a business partner of mine. I was fascinated by the other members of the Theatre Upstairs Committee. 'Whatever brings them here?' I thought. 'They know nothing, but *nothing* about the theatre.' I am not suggesting they were unintelligent, but their knowledge of this world was as much as mine would have been if I had joined a committee concerned with nuclear energy. But then not all the world is nuclear energy struck, while all the world *is* stage struck.

Our Chairman was Lois Sieff, Edward Sieff's widow, an enthusiastic, eternally young American, very anxious to contribute to the artistic life of London. She was able to arrange expensive fund-raising parties at Marks & Spencer's head office, where she was, quite naturally, the Hostess with the Mostest. Champagne and elaborate canapés were served by the excellent head office staff, and immensely boring speeches from a platform raised high were given by rich ladies, very well-meaning, but hoping to make the point that nice, clean shows should come back to our theatre. I thought I heard Robin's voice: 'Don't be beastly, Angela, stop laughing, the theatre needs the money!'

On our board too was immensely generous Mrs Henni Gestetner, and decorative Sonia, Lady Melchet, who, I understand, was a Justice of the Peace. She was charming and her son was a Socialist peer. She did such a good job for the Royal Court, and I would like to have got to know her better. I could have asked her a lot of questions if I had made the time because I was immensely curious about her. I would love to have found out if she herself had ever experienced the rough and seedy side and the penury so often known by the people that she was judging. She is an extraordinarily attractive woman and has made a great contribution to the artistic scene in London in the seventies and eighties.

I remember Drusilla Beyfus, an experienced journalist, married to the theatre critic Milton Shulman. She seemed so nice and I wondered if she was there because she agreed with her husband, or simply longed to disagree with him. For a while there was Ariana Stassinopoulos, a very tall, decorative young Greek woman. I understand she had distinguished herself at university, but she had more often hit the headlines as a great friend of Bernard Levin. She was most confident and arrogant and made full use of her handsomeness and height and her rather strange Greek accent. She was different from the rest of us, and this was rather agreeable to her, it seemed. I am sure she must have been to plays at the Royal Court Theatre with Bernard Levin, but she gave nothing of this away.

What I do remember (and am, of course, ashamed at being so petty – I must have been jealous of her youth and beauty and self-possession) was that she wore a cloak and that, after one meeting, she swept past me down the steps outside the theatre, catching me in the swirl of this garment. I was flattened against the board announcing the next play and felt rather cross, but this turned to pleasure when I saw, as she went on her way with great speed, that both her stockings had bad ladders in them. She was human, after all – quite a relief!

Of course the Committee was large enough to merit a whole book. I used to think about Anthony Trollope and what he would have observed, so much more than I could

– I who sat there for the wrong reasons, a distraught woman looking for something to do.

On an afternoon, sitting at one of these meetings, it came to me that I was making no contribution among these well-meaning, sincere people, ready to use their energies – and often their cheque books – to make possible the continuation of something with which I was totally out of sympathy. The best of the Royal Court Theatre was dead, as dead as those who had created it.

I had not been ready, until that moment, to face that what is past is past, that a strong team – George Devine, the all important guru, Neville Blond, the Chairman, who could have chaired anything brilliantly regardless of whether he knew the subject or not, and Robin Fox, the middle man – were all dead. Their ghosts were in this little room for me, but only for me. Elaine Blond, the late Lord Mark's younger sister and my friend of a lifetime, continued to give Marks & Spencer support, although she was not in sympathy with the concept of this theatre, and never had been. She did not like it, and neither did she like anyone concerned with it.

A good story against her, but which amused her very much, was when many do-gooders, helped in the main part by the generosity of Marks & Spencer's, refurbished the theatre throughout. George Devine proudly took her to see it, naïvely expecting praise. She looked around carefully at the immense amount of work that had been done and said, 'I still don't think much of the ladies' lavatories.'

The main reason I attended the meetings at all was to enjoy a laugh. On one side of the little room, jammed together like sardines, would be the squares, totally hostile towards the group jammed together on the other side, the new management hierarchy, headed by a young man who looked bored and antagonistic, called Max Stafford-Clark (whom I am told is a very good director). I wondered to myself, 'Did he know that it was Elaine's money, and the money of other generous capitalists present, that made it possible for him and his team to be working at the Royal Court at all?' I do know the answer to that, but I did see what appeared to be a very cross young man, devoid of manners, and with a chip on his shoulder.

On this afternoon, when I decided that further attendance on my part would be useless, I thought, 'That's it, no manners, and a chip on their shoulders' had applied all along to a group of brilliant young people who were discovered, drawn together and kept and inspired to work together by the genius of George Devine. Even to tough, sophisticated Robin Fox, who worked for nothing on the administrative side from the day he met him until the day he died because he believed that what George was doing for the theatre, for writers and directors and actors and for audiences, was of vital importance. The main thing was that he loved the man – he was not alone in this, for George was loved by all who came in close working contact with him.

George and I never really became friends, but our paths were linked for a number of years through Robin, who became agent to many talented people brought into his life through George – to name but a few, Tony Richardson, Anthony Page, William Gaskill, and that great writer John Osborne. I used to think of them as furious near-geniuses. Most of them have mellowed. I wonder if talent mellows when anger dies down: is furious aggression, a loathing of conventional society or of civilized behaviour, a creative force or a dangerous force in itself? That play of John Osborne's, *Look Back in Anger*, altered the whole concept of the theatre as it had been known for many years. It seemed to unleash a fury that must have been simmering a long time. John's great talent was born for others to follow suit – and then on to the scene came writers like Arnold Wesker, David Storey, Edward Bond and many more.

I must not exaggerate and say that I never enjoyed performances in those days because, although I often had reservations, productions like Lindsay Anderson's *In Celebration* by David Storey were handled with sensitivity and a visual sense which I shall never forget. Another man who could, and never can, do anything wrong by me is John Dexter. I particularly think of his production of Arnold Wesker's *Roots* and the electrifying performance he got from Joan Plowright – then a young actress just starting out.

There is no doubt that Robin's passion in life was the Royal Court Theatre and everything concerned with it, and a play he liked so much and I loathed was Edward Bond's *Saved*. I saw nothing new in the so-called under-privileged being bestially cruel, but then I had been very, very poor as a young girl in Glasgow, and learned, as anyone would, a few sharp lessons.

I was amused – dare I say even proud – that I was giving such a performance that the Royal Court group appeared to think of me as an over-privileged appendage of Robin's – that is, if they noticed me at all. Such was Robin's love for and interest in this theatre that a bit of him died when George Devine did. He scarcely ever showed emotion, but I still remember the day he heard the news. He was in anguish, and his eyes were full of tears.

Around the time that I learned that Robin's illness was terminal – that he was not just unwell, and that no treatment could save him – he was making a telephone call to New York about John Gielgud and Ralph Richardson, who were going there to act in David Storey's play *Home*, again directed by Lindsay Anderson. This had started life in Sloane Square. Robin was on the telephone making the deal, getting cross, I expect, and then he had a fit. That was the beginning of the very end for him – except that he did not want to die at all, this would have been the way out that he would have chosen. It took longer than that.

The last time he ever went to the theatre, thin and fragile, a ghost of himself, it was to see this play, which had transferred to the West End. We had a box and when we went backstage to see John Gielgud, that kind man had changed and was ready and waiting. Robin's favourite whisky was put out for him, and they sat and talked, and I listened and the theatre was quiet. No fireman came to tell us we must soon leave. John Gielgud seemed to have all the time in the world.

When finally we got back in our car to go home, we fell silent. We both remembered that first conversation between two stage-struck young people, each of us overwhelmed with enthusiasm for an actor called John Gielgud in a play called *Richard of Bordeaux*. Another full cycle had come round. Robin knew he would never see him again. He accepted that and so much more. I am told acceptance makes things easier. I am not so sure.

So much has been written about the Royal Court. Serious books have been published, the work of people who have taken a great deal of trouble, who have done research. But they were not there. The Royal Court, and all concerned with it, was about magic. George Devine and his team made just that.

It succeeded because he had the guts and staying power; no matter what field you choose to be in, that makes the winner. It is typified, for example, by the champions at Wimbledon. All the players are magnificent, but it is the one who achieves a balance with his mental and physical powers who holds up that huge cup. George Devine had these gifts and they killed him.

*

It was Robin's friend, Lord Harewood, who supplied a lot of the jigsaw pieces I was looking for, because he helped me on my way back to normality. He was a born teacher and he brought into my life, as he has into the lives of hundreds of people in the audience, an appreciation of music and opera. I am still an ignorant member of the audience, but am ever aware of the pleasure that his efforts on my behalf have given me and, as long as I can hear, it will never leave me, for my enjoyment of music and opera increases all the time. I was such a beginner when he took me on that he used to have to tell me the story of the opera before the curtain went up, advise me what records to listen to, and select the passages to which I should really pay the most attention.

That was not all. Patricia, his lovely Australian wife, invited me to Harewood. They hardly knew me. Robin had been his friend, but the nervous, apprehensive widow became the guest at a music festival in which they were involved. I had to muck in, get listening, or go home. I stayed, enjoyed everything hugely and started to learn late in life more than school had ever taught me. I also became involved in football with them when Leeds were playing – George being Chairman of that Club – so I now know what my grandsons are on about.

I hope George Harewood was not too ashamed of me when he took me to see his team play football. He could have been quite pleased when I sipped afternoon tea with the wives of the power boys behind the team. 'Yes, I am proud of my boys. How kind of you to say that you loved that performance . . . Yes, they love soccer. It's their favourite sport. They will be green with envy when they hear where I have been today and that I have met you all . . . Yes, I'd love another cucumber sandwich.'

But when I got back to my seat among the privileged few, I sat next to the Harewoods' son, Mark, then about fourteen when I first attended matches. He showed me the programme, explained the sides, told me the names of all the players, as much as he could of what he had learned from his father about their characters and their capabilities, but, as the whistle blew and the ball got its first kick, I was shouting and screaming like the most violent of the hooligans.

I enjoyed the skill and controlled fury so much, but in a flash I had forgotten everything that I had ever been told, even the names of the teams playing, let alone whom I should support. I just yelled. It was all such lunatic fun and the frenzy around me so wild that I do not think anyone cared that a grandmother had become so carried away, although she had no idea why she was there, or even who she was.

I was so grateful for all these good times that, naturally,

I wanted to do something in return for the Harewoods, an opportunity which I took up with gusto, and, if I look back, I think with outrageous nerve, because I had so little equipment or experience for the task I volunteered to undertake. But I pressed ahead and I got much more out of the effort than I ever put into it, so that I have never for one moment regretted my audacity. I became Vice-Chairman of the English National Opera Benevolent Fund, of which Jennie Lee was Chairman. If it is 'never too late to learn', then off I went, and did I learn? Jennie Lee had been, in Robin's opinion (never a political one), the best Minister for the Arts contemporary England had ever had. She wasted no time, took a meeting like a clear-headed man, and left the Committee in no doubt about what was wanted and what each of them could do about it . . . and they did.

The huge Committee of the ENO was not very different from that of the Theatre Upstairs. What did we all arrange to do? We organized gala first nights at other theatres where women dragged their unwilling husbands to plays they loathed, having paid fortunes for the seats because these ladies wanted to see and be seen. Most of these people were very rich, had charitable trusts, and were often conscientious and generous.

The day I reached the height of unpopularity was the day when, as Vice-Chairman, I spoke. In that role it appears that this was a most unseemly thing to do. I said that what we wanted from all present was money. How about just asking them to write cheques, and then those who were less fortunate than us would benefit, and the cause we represented would flourish? After a long, possibly anxious, working day, men could enjoy a quiet dinner and relax by the fireside instead of being dragged to something they did not want to see.

No way. What an unacceptable thought. My days as Vice-Chairman of a distinguished charity were drawing to an inevitable close.

Looking back, I see all my 'good works' as selfish and rather absurd, but it was a case of looking for something to do. Even more, when Robin was alive, it was a means of running away from the difficult side of our marriage that I did not want to face. I used working for charity to boost my morale, to try to assure myself that I was of use somewhere. That medicine failed both before and after he died.

George Harewood and his wife Patricia extended wonderful friendship to me, but with the ENO he had vast problems. His love for and knowledge of music, greater in both cases than anything I have ever encountered or ever will, was not going to solve his biggest problem, and that was where to find the money for this opera house that was enjoying a huge success – largely in my opinion due to his efforts. I understood the problem, wanted to do all I could, because I soon learned how much it meant to him and, indeed, to an ever-growing, enthusiastic audience. But really we were beaten at the start. Probably due to his background, money was a dirty word, it was abhorrent to him ever to ask for it. I knew how to get it but the methods I would have to have employed would have been useless unless he had given his blessing to a more direct approach, and this I knew he would never do. It was very frustrating, very disappointing, but I had to laugh because this was why I admired him – indeed loved these two very great friends.

I was also on the general money-raising committee of the

ENO, with some of the most distinguished men in London, and had the Huge Pleasure of Taking Tea with our Chairman, who was, in fact, the Chairman of the London Stock Exchange, Sir Nicholas Goodison.

As I sailed up and up and up in the elevator to the top floor of the Stock Exchange, I thought I had died and I had felt no pain and here I was on my way to Heaven, the last thing I expected. I must have been a better person than I realized, my efforts had not been wasted. The illusion did not fade immediately because the beauty of London seen from the windows all round his magnificent office is one of the wonders of the modern world. We had China tea and cucumber sandwiches. How wonderful, how amazing of this brilliant, cultured, erudite, important, scholarly man actually to find time to give me tea. How impertinent of me to enjoy taking the time of this immensely important human being.

Despite his elevated status, Sir Nicholas looked like a tow-headed schoolboy, his wrists seemed bony and I always thought he wore a short-sleeved sports shirt under his jacket as cuffs were never visible. I was quite incredulous; what was a man in his position doing asking me, of all people, how to raise money?

I set about the problem in my usual, rather bossy way and tried to explain to him that galas were a bore, and that I felt that communication between the very rich and the aristocratic over a civilized dinner table was more likely to do the trick. I told him that what I had observed was that the very rich, particularly if they were self-made, longed to know the aristocracy, who still held all the keys, and the aristocracy usually longed to know the very rich – because they did not know how to make very aristocratic ends meet. There were final doors the rich always wanted to open.

But Sir Nicholas could not be convinced that giving dinner parties to get interested people together would solve ENO's problems. In such a way did my original idea to help the Benevolent Fund fall on stony ground. Our chat over the tea cups in this home in the sky of the Chairman of the London Stock Exchange was brief. I had time to wonder how this wild-eyed, untidy intellectual, who was internationally admired for his connoisseurship of barometers and clocks and porcelain, among other things, also had the drive to merit a position of such huge importance in the material world. I have no doubt at all that I was wrong, but I kept thinking, 'What a square peg in a round hole.'

As the elevator, which I had thought was possibly going to lead me to the pearly gates, plunged earthwards after my visit had come to an end, I recalled an awful evening we had all spent after a very demanding performance given by the ENO Company. The singers and musicians had been invited by their Chairman to cold supper high up in a shabby room at the top of the Coliseum. The singers were tired, the evening was flat, and, for no reason that I can fathom, balloons were let off among this jaded company. The real enthusiast in collecting and popping the balloons with a pin was their distinguished host. It surprised me to see yet another side of this energetic man, and I sat thinking rather ruefully how I wished he could have had the vision to persuade the owners of the Coliseum to renovate their shabby building and so help these fine singers acquire a theatre worthy of their art. What a difficult task this would have been. I wondered if he had ever taken in the disgusting condition of the dressing-rooms, for instance, from which these singers emerged often to uplift and inspire their audience.

*

Sometimes when I was fortunate enough after a performance to sit in an expensive restaurant or someone's elegant dining-room, listening to the talk about singing and interpretation, my own stresses felt pretty unmanageable. I did my best to fix my mind and concentrate on what was being said. Patrons of the opera and theatre think they have the knowledge to express informed opinions and are forever giving their views. I recall Robin once having to listen *ad infinitum* to a banker's interminable criticism of some play, and showing his irritation. He often felt it, but only once in our life together do I remember him retaliating. He said, 'Let us speak of something else, or I, too, will talk on a subject of which I am totally ignorant – banking.'

How fortunate ENO has been. When I arrived the Chairman was Lord Goodman, who has been succeeded by Lord Harewood. It was Lord Goodman who set the ball rolling for this marvellous company, in the face of heavy odds that would have left a lesser man putting on his slippers and relaxing by his fireside. Although I could never boast that I have ever been a friend of Lord Goodman's, I enjoyed his chairmanship at meetings. I doubt he ever knew whether I was in the room. I have observed him quite superficially play many different parts. He is a large, lumbering man, heavy jowled, beetle-browed above black, watching, boot-button eyes, slow to move physically, but the speed of his mind is astonishing.

I knew at first hand that he was very kind to Jennie Lee. His friendship was very important to her when the chips were down. He seemed to me to be a most concerned and loyal man.

He has a finger in so many pies, and important pies at that; huge legal problems are well known to be grist to his mill, and I also know from other friends who have benefited from his kind side that he has time for small people and young people who are in trouble with the law, sometimes entirely through their own fault.

In particular I believe he was the guru to the high-powered on the left of the political scene, but whenever I watch this huge figure dominating the social scene, he seems to be just observing like a sleepy bulldog, waiting to bite if necessary. I was interested that he always chose to accompany him on these occasions exceedingly beautiful women with reputations for wit and charm, but epitomizing, I thought, a few of the less attractive characteristics of the right wing, coming from a class I rather felt to be the over-privileged. In some ways I found it a bit old-fashioned. This, of course, could well be jealousy on my part. As I have said, he never took the faintest notice of me. Standing with these lovely ladies, even listening to their problems and social banter, must have been a pleasant form of relaxation for the Cyrano de Bergerac of his day.

I never heard Arnold Goodman say anything that was not interesting, and he was often very wise. My husband served on the Arts Council with him when he was Chairman. His interest in the arts was constant, and to the musical world important. Would I say he had a great influence one way or the other in the theatre? Not particularly. But then for this fine brain there were so many fish to fry. In his own field he was a star, and I have always had a passion for the brightest and the best. I spend my life like someone looking up into a summer sky, remembering as a child the words 'Look at those twinkling stars'. What I really feel is that they are looking down on us, and very often winking.

*

I suppose deciding to work for the National Adoption Society was the nearest to being serious about something that I could ever get. When I joined, it was a voluntary organization and our dedicated Chairman was Mrs Gerald (now Lady) Glover. We were what the popular press call privileged. I remember attending the first meeting after being well and truly vetted to see if I was suitable for the job. I went into a pokey little room in Manchester Square. There were more rich women with titles jammed round a small table than I could believe possible. They fitted the label 'privileged', especially as used by those with lefty sympathies, to a tee. But a harder working, more highly qualified group of women would be hard to meet. We attended committee meetings at this Manchester Square office to report on what we had been doing.

There were very many different sides to the work, and we had to take a turn at all of them, such as interviewing those who wished to adopt a child, and identifying anything they had in common with the children who might become available. The idea was to place a child with people who were similar in every way, physically and mentally, to the natural parents. Our job was to be as calm and as observant as possible, compassionate, and yet detached – the most difficult frame of mind for the inexperienced amateur, because the couple who sat before us were like people on trial. They had failed to have a child, which was the one thing they both desired more than anything else on earth, but they, too, had to present a calm and balanced façade.

This ordeal did not take place once, but three or four times, at least, before they were told that they were even being considered, and then they had to wait and wait and wait again, perhaps, for a suitable child to appear who complemented their physical appearance, their family background, the type of work they had chosen – in fact who resembled their own personalities as closely as was humanly possible. I used to wonder how the whole process went on at all, because for all concerned the situation was very nearly impossibly difficult.

The task was made even more difficult because quite often we knew very little about the natural father. Then we interviewed emotionally distraught girls who felt they must arrange for the child to be given to a stranger a week or so after its life had begun.

Some of our time was spent on long days in the courtroom, because until a child has been six months with the adoptive parents, the natural mother can reclaim it. Battles for this could be tough, often with agonizing decisions, which were up to the judge.

Reports in detail had to be given about the well-being or otherwise of babies who had been adopted through us. That meant visits all over England to the homes of the new parents to look closely at them and the baby, the house and everything that concerned the health of the child. Absolutely nothing had to go unobserved. This soon became a role I took on, always accompanied, I have to admit, by somebody more experienced than myself. We hunted in pairs and I went with someone with whom I have established a great friendship, and whom I met through joining the Society: Lady Gloria Flower. She was typical of all the women on that committee – experienced, compassionate and dedicated to the well-being of the children who passed through our hands.

I failed totally on one side of the work. The natural mother had to come to Manchester Square with her baby of a few weeks old. She had had it long enough to love the child, as every normal woman does. She would be shown into one small room. One of the committee had to take the child from her, and hand it to a strange man and woman, waiting anxiously in another small room only a few feet away. Immediately, all the necessary work having been done in advance, they were able to disappear carrying the baby that they had so passionately longed for – they carried in their arms a dream come true.

As a working member of the National Adoption Society, I had to learn to take on this job. I could not do it then or now or ever, and so I failed, and I suspect I was never taken quite seriously after that. I did not feel too bad about this failure. It made me help with all the energy I possessed to raise money for our home in Northampton, where girls went for a few weeks before the baby was due. There they made the acquaintance of other girls in exactly the same position, and also with young mothers bringing their babies back from hospital where, if all was normal, they would remain for twenty-four hours. After the baby was born, mother and child were together for several weeks.

Obviously I was the last person who should have become involved in taking the child away from its natural parent, because I really felt happiness at the many times a girl would change her mind and never part with her baby. Quite often her parents turned up, parents who had been ashamed of their girl, but took one look at their grandchild and all differences were resolved.

If I made any contribution, it was because I was an ideas person, and people much more able than me carried out some thoughts that I had. I certainly had been one of the first people to enthuse over the idea of this home, and I felt very strongly that it should be made possible – whenever both parents were willing – that the natural father should be able to see the mother and the child whose birth could never have happened without him. I got a great kick when, sometimes, marriages were arranged. Happy endings are rare, but I am always looking for them.

For this very small, practical part of the scene that I had helped to make possible, I felt rather pleased. We were all good at different aspects of the work. It was a successful, well-run organization. Can the same be said now? Well, it has been taken over by the Social Services, and with what results? The National Adoption Society, which had arranged homes and security for thousands of children, is no more.

Very few cases were ever straightforward and easy. Sometimes when we had done all the necessary work, the new parents arrived to take over their offspring, took one look and decided in no way was it what they wanted and turned on their heels. So the baby would have to go into temporary care in a foster home.

One moment the prospective mother was a nine-to-five, hard-working, childless woman, and suddenly she was summoned to Manchester Square, from where she would walk away clutching her strange son or daughter. I was always very touched by the fact that I knew from seeing their homes that the nursery where the child was to be taken had been ready, down to the last safety pin, for a long, long time. It had been silent, and now there would be screams for years to come.

Despite my suspicion of 'do-gooders', I favour the concept of the voluntary charity worker. I help Irene, Lady Astor, raise money for the Sunshine Fund for Blind Babies, something I have done for many years now. The list of names on this committee comprises the grandest in *Debrett*, but on the day of our annual fair, on go the aprons, the sleeves are rolled up, and a long day is tackled. I only run the raffle, so there is time to hear snatches about the daily lives of these women.

When the last member of the public leaves after the long day, the huge hall we have been working in is a dirty, grotty shambles. Where, we wonder, are the people paid to maintain the place? Gone home, of course, on the dot of five o'clock, paid, I believe, by the taxpayer. So it is these privileged ladies who sweep and clean and clear up all the debris and never leave until the place looks like the proverbial new pin. Oh yes, it is the voluntary worker for me!

5

Wedding in the Strand

In March 1974 a very different marriage from that of James was arranged.

On Robert's twenty-first birthday we gave a highly theatrical party at Ockenden Cottage. Among the guests, of course, was Robert's girlfriend, Lois Daine, her and Tom Bell's twelve-year-old son Aran, and their sheepdog.

But one person who was most polite to me was a very unusually dressed girl with good eyes, who was wearing black from head to toe and sported a very eccentric hat, with a feather sticking up in the air. She came and sat with me and I asked her who she was. She told me her name was Celestia Sporborg. She made herself agreeable and was quite obviously from what my mother would have termed 'a good background'. I was rather intrigued by her. I asked, 'What brings you here today?'

'I'm going to marry Robert.'

'I'm not so sure about that. You see that girl over there?' pointing to Lois, 'he is living with her and they seem to be happy.'

'I am going to marry him,' she replied. I was incredulous at this statement but I learned over the years that if Celestia announced that she was going to do something, I must consider it done.

She did marry Robert, within a year, with a magnificent ceremony at the Savoy Chapel, and the wedding breakfast in the River Room at the Savoy, as splendid as only that hotel can provide.

Remembering how scornful I had been concerning James and Mary's wedding, from which I had not come out well, Robert's wedding gave a boost to my flagging morale. I admit I was pleased and relieved that my youngest son appeared ready to embrace the security of the establishment, and it interests me now, that when I should have reached a state of maturity, I was still making mistakes and had much to learn.

Celestia's father, Harry Sporborg, was a very disting- uished man. From the time we met until he died in 1985, he was a wise and good friend to me, as he had been all his life to many people. I remember with amusement that he gave a bit of a jolt to an area of naïvety in me, born of my determination to turn geese into swans. I realized this on the occasion of inviting him and his wife, Mary, to dine with me at Eaton Square to celebrate our children's engagement. I was determined to show them that their daughter had made the right choice and that Robert came from what they would call 'the right background'. Needless to say, as I was a very experienced party giver, the food was right. Berry Bros and Rudd were consulted so that the wine and the port (I had learned that Harry was a connoisseur in this field) left nothing to be desired. Expensive extra staff, who did the dinner party rounds nightly in the Square, were engaged, while Betty was at the helm in the kitchen. So over-anxious was I to get the details right that even the flowers were arranged by Pulbrook and Gould, with Lady Pulbrook herself looking in on her way home to give the nod of approval. I could quite easily have brought them from my own garden and done them myself.

The party was not to be big. The guests were the objects of the exercise, Robert and Celestia of course and, to support them, Edward and Joanna, who, on instruction from me, arrived on time for once, took one look at the over-decorated flat and remarked that I had gone off my head. After very careful thought about my guest list, I had asked my old friend, Marcus Sieff, and Lily, his wife. Marcus was no longer the boy with whom I had had so much fun, but a man very much to be reckoned with, deferred to with very good reason by men of many nations. Since Robin died, I had not seen quite so much of him, but nothing had affected our friendship. He was Edward's godfather and had been Robin's oldest and closest friend. I thought he would add weight to the Fox team.

The evening was a disaster. It started with a flourish as Marcus arrived with plain-clothes men to guard his life, something I had not anticipated. But this was justified as his very nice and gentle uncle, Teddy Sieff, had lately nearly met his death when an assassin had burst into his house and shot him when he was in his bathroom.

The last arrivals were Harry and Mary Sporborg, she handsome, elegant, rather frightening, Harry dignified and quiet. If he was aware in any way of the armed guards, he would have been the last man to react as, in the war, he had been one of the heads of Special Operations Executive.

We had champagne in the drawing-room and dinner was announced. Harry was on my right, and Marcus on my left. I do not suppose they recalled what had happened a moment after they left the flat, but I shall, with amusement, for the rest of my life, because immediately an appalling row flared up between the two men. Used as I was to manoeuvring social chat, I was beaten at the start.

The disagreement was about the Shah of Persia. My knowledge of the impending political problems in his country was limited to unavoidable references in the press as Persia – which is Iran now – and the surrounding countries were being given more and more space. I did know that Marcus and Lily had been the Shah's guests several times.

I was jolted out of my role as the relaxed Belgravia hostess by a real slanging match. What lay behind it I can only guess. Anyway, it took place between two very powerful men with totally different, nevertheless well-founded opinions on the subject. Harry Sporborg, of Swedish extraction, was clearly not impressed by the Shah and his regime, but Marcus, more worldly, had a pro-Shah attitude not perhaps unconnected with his practical and national interests, but that water was too deep for me even to speculate in. In fact, it was a time for me to listen and, above all, know nothing. It was with amazement that I realized such high feelings were leading to near loss of temper on both their parts. And so they rocked the boat of an innocent social occasion. I was disappointed, of course, that the delicious dinner was ignored, although the wine went down all right. But the whole object of the exercise went up in smoke.

I remember that, as hostess, I never had to catch the

ladies' eyes and lead them to the drawing-room, thus leaving the men to the port and huge cigars and what they were wont to call civilized conversation. The party broke up as soon as Betty's famous soufflé Grand Marnier had been nervously pushed around the plates and the Foxes were suddenly on their own again, glad, I think, that we were not members of the international political scene, but simply a family connected with the world of the theatre.

We all repaired to the kitchen where the young ones did credit to the remains of Betty's soufflé, now, like us, rather flat. We helped with the washing up, finished the drink I had bought for the party and started to laugh, and, I am afraid, did imitations of our important guests. I remember feeling sorry for Celestia at the course that the evening had taken. I had hoped it would be a happier occasion for her and for her family. Her father was a fine and serious man of integrity, and she had decided to become part of a family who appeared to laugh at almost everything. I never succeeded in explaining to her that, when there was a real crisis, be it our country going to war, or in matters of friendship, our fundamental values were the same as her father's. I should have been able to explain to her it was ourselves we found it difficult to take seriously.

*

As I have said, I was to learn that if Celestia ever said she was going to do something – anything – then she did it, starting with the unlikely announcement that she was going to marry Robert. She stormed through life and she stormed into marriage, and the greatest distress I have ever known was witnessing her deep, incredulous unhappiness when the marriage broke up. I think I have said almost too often that the mother, mother-in-law or any relation who is very close finds it impossible, if they are honest, to understand the emotional turmoil of the young and are idiotic if they think there is a single thing that they can do except leave the door open.

She fell in love with Robert – no doubt anywhere that this was true; very often her strength worked greatly to his advantage. She worked without stint on his behalf. She became, and is, a brilliant casting director in the theatre and in films. Her name is continually seen on the titles in the cinema and on the television screen. She is very shrewd and aware of actors and their potential to play certain parts. Also, she is the most discreet woman regarding her work that I shall ever meet. She has a good business brain. I often asked her advice on matters concerning money because I was always in difficulties. What she said was sound and sensible.

I hope one day we shall be friends again and I shall be able to continue where we left off. We do meet. I am very fond of her, although it is not easy for her to like me. After all, I am Robert's mother. She was no one's enemy, but she was her own. Her love for Robert was so real, so over-riding, so possessive. For twelve years they were inseparable and the most loving parents of their three children. They had a lovely home which she had found and bought most cleverly, but Robert had no study of his own. He could not even make business calls in the evening, so essential as much of his work involved contact with American companies, because a boisterous young family making a row well known to all parents dominated everything, and Celestia, the ever-loving mother, never said, 'Belt up.' They went to bed much later than my children ever did, and then their mother, with her amazing energy, was ready to do the town – the jet-set scene – spending the rest of the night in the smart night spots. Something had to snap and, finally, it was Robert. He was a workaholic, worn to a frazzle by the life they were leading, but never can it be said his wife did not love him – she did, in her way, too much.

No personal unhappiness in anyone I have ever known compares with the despair I witnessed in my daughter-in-law. I felt pain for her and I understood totally her isolated misery. She never was a girl to communicate easily, and I think she was so sure of him, her feeling for him was so intense, that not even imagination warned her of the tragedy. To her it *was* tragedy that hit her.

I took on the role of the distraught grandmother, identified the children's plight with the hang-ups of my own childhood. I have learned a sharp lesson. The stress and agony I let take me over were absolutely unnecessary. Children are bound to encounter unhappiness, and if it is not real they will concoct it.

The three children of Robert and Celestia are healthy, and are resilient in the way that only children can be. There are bad days, black moods, but they are beautiful, naughty, and very normal. They love school, where they do very well at work and games, and have hordes of friends. The divorce or separation of their parents is something most of these children know too. So I must learn to stop being the pained, wistful grandmother and try finding a sense of humour, sit back and enjoy the scene. After all, to laugh must be the only thing I can do.

PART TWO

6

Rough Going

'I never give them roast pork.' He doesn't like it.

'I never wear pink.' It's a colour he hates.

'I couldn't ask the Smiths for dinner.' They bore him.

'I couldn't accept the Grafs' invitation to ski with them in Bavaria.' He hated the Germans in the war and he sees no reason to alter his opinion of them now.

When I am with women friends of my age group, who still have husbands to hide behind, it makes me wish I was going to live long enough to be a fly on the wall so that I could listen to the young feminists of today when they are middle-aged. Perhaps they will not sound quite so idiotic. It is true that those of my generation of whom I speak were sent to so-called 'good schools', but educational standards were totally different from today.

I learned good manners, to observe and consider other people and not to take myself too seriously. Quite a number of my contemporaries, getting the same treatment, have become very distinguished women in their own right, often making valuable contributions to the lives of their fellow men.

My mother was uneducated by today's standards and so am I, but, like her, I know the importance of education. I am fascinated by the full programme at every level that my granddaughters have to cope with and seem to enjoy. I even confess to feeling a bit envious. But will they be any better equipped to deal with the emotional problems which figure so largely in the lives of all women?

It is now nearly eighteen years since Robin died. They have been full years and I would be a liar and a hypocrite if I do not admit that what success my sons have achieved gives me pleasure. Of course that is only part of the picture, and when we are referred to in the press or by friends as being a 'successful family', I wonder who they can be talking about. No doubt this is because my half-baked efforts to find out what I could do that would be faintly useful to anyone did not seem to be bearing much fruit. I was saddled with quite a task since a great part of me went with Robin, as those who have lost a partner of a lifetime will know. It is like standing over and looking into a vast, empty chasm, and something is telling you that you have got to try and fill it up.

I would have given anything in the world just to have had the rows and misunderstandings back, and even the awful and cruel things we said to each other at times, the confrontations, the furies. I do not really know what I think love is, but I would rather he was here to enrage me than be on good terms with any other man I have ever met. This does not mean that I do not like men – I do; but, although Robin could be wicked, he was – and all his friends agree with me – clever, shrewd and morally and physically courageous, qualities he had in abundance. He was a real man.

Looking back I see that grief is a most selfish emotion. I was absolutely convinced that only I knew such depths of unhappiness at Robin's dying. How stupid and how selfish. I know that his two great friends, Robert Morley and Michael Sieff, were both profoundly unhappy when the chapter in the life that they had shared with him came to an end. Of course life went on for both of them, but I feel it can never have been the same without 'Foxglove', as Robert Morley always called him, or Bob Fox, the term of endearment that Michael Sieff always used. I think I loved both of these men and now perhaps wish I had been a better friend to both of them and more understanding and not so overwhelmed with self-pity. That is such a boring, selfish emotion.

When Robin was in the Issels Clinic they cared enough about us both to come every weekend. They wanted to do everything in their power to help and comfort him and, looking back, I confess I could never have stayed the course without the support of these two good friends.

Robert Morley always had his splendid wife, Joan, and his children to go back to. Michael Sieff blotted out the past by marrying a very pretty young woman called Elizabeth, whom he met when she was nursing first his aunt Miriam and then his father in their last illnesses with great expertise. She was young and lovely and full of life and I think the end of his life was very happy. He became a devoted husband and father and I used to tease him because he was such a different man from the stage-door Johnny who had brought me flowers after the show and taken me out to such good suppers.

He was Robin's sole executor, a role he had taken on when Robin, knowing that he was dying, asked if Michael would mind the responsibility. He accepted at once. When the task became a reality he hated everything to do with it and it was real agony for him to have to attend to this sad business. I did not feel cross when the Estate, as it was called, appeared terribly complicated and actually took many years to settle, because that is not my attitude to money, then or now. The reason I was endlessly harassed and worried was because at first it appeared that Robin had left more than an adequate amount, but I was, in fact, completely broke. I was utterly astounded at what I had to learn.

Michael was a very sensitive man and I do not think for a moment that he knew how distraught and confused I felt. It is the last thing he would have wanted. But I sometimes think we only understand what we have lived through and to be hard up had never been his lot. Michael's father, Israel Sieff, and his uncle, Simon Marks, heads of the vast Marks & Spencer empire, made it impossible for their young relatives to know what being short of money meant. And so he was not insensitive about my plight, just utterly unaware of the difficulties involved.

In retrospect I see I have only myself to blame at feeling distressed. I had no great belief in money, I knew all about how that could disappear, so when I picked up the *Evening Standard* and turned the pages casually and my eye was caught by a short sentence, I was not as flabbergasted as some of my more well-heeled friends would have been. I turned the pages idly, knowing I must chuck it aside and go and get dressed as I had been invited to a smart dinner party. I came across the words, 'The Estate of Robin Fox, Theatrical Impresario – NIL.' After so many years of misunderstanding, sometimes on my part, it hardly came as a surprise.

I remember walking to the window of our beautiful drawing-room in Eaton Square, the room that Robin and I had so enjoyed buying pictures for and furnishing. We loved this room, although neither of us thought of it as a home where we could relax completely and become private people. That happened at Cuckfield and Cornwall, but this room had marvellous views of a very rich part of London. We had St Peter's, Eaton Square, on our right, and we looked through magnificent trees, sharply uphill, which rather surprised me, to Belgrave Square. I knew that this was one of the last times that I would stand at this window.

*

Entertainment is now very much a business – an industry. It has gone through the same changes as sport, but real talent survives whoever manipulates the purse strings. There will always be a great deal of grumbling from the artists themselves – that seems to me quite normal and not unhealthy – and surely art has always needed over the ages the boys with the money in the bank to be patrons?

I learnt how rough the entertainment industry can be, and later knew how foolish I had been, when I encouraged Robin to leave the Music Corporation of America because he did not like the actors he represented being treated roughly, unless they engendered exactly the right noises in the box office. He was a tough businessman on their behalf, but he really loved the people whom he represented and he probably should have stayed the course with MCA, the firm he had joined with the help and sound advice of Simon Marks, a far greater realist than either of us. He knew we were penniless after the war, but that we wanted to educate our children and to build up our family life.

When Robin left MCA – encouraged by me because he was not happy – he sacrificed a very big pension which, of course, would have made my life very much easier. I do not regret any of this. He was in love with the theatre. He put on a number of plays and reviews and some of them were successful. He was in partnership with his dearest friend, Robert Morley, and they had a lot of fun. I am not sure how they managed it, but in a year or so the Robin Fox Partnership went bust. Fate put out a kindly hand and Leslie Grade appeared on the scene and said he would like Robin to join him and create a 'straight' theatre side to his business. Leslie was at that time the greatest of the variety agents. Robin did ask my views on this. Having met Leslie, I was tremendously in favour of the venture, and so the Grade Organization was formed and Robin became extremely successful in the material sense. With Leslie he was happy. He had fun. He forgot to grumble and I ceased to hear the mournful phrase which had haunted me through the years at MCA: 'I live vicariously through the talent of other people.' Leslie was brilliant and they were right for each other. It was a perfect partnership. And then, at the height of their success, Leslie suffered a cerebral haemorrhage. He did not die. He lived a few more years. I was in Paris with one of my sisters when Robin telephoned me with the news and I knew for certain that at this moment the joy and the laughter had ceased for him.

I was right, though others will not have seen it that way.

He became head of his own agency, the International Famous Agency. This was very successful too. But he was a sad man in private, and he was fifty-five when he told me one evening on arriving home that he had a shadow on his lung and that he was going to die. He did just that. It took nine months.

There was one way in which he differed from other theatrical agents. His clients were his friends. Above all, he understood them, however difficult they were, and he really loved them. Many famous people knew this and felt it to be true and they come and tell me so today. When he died, life was never quite the same for them. He was deeply loved in return, and I benefited from this then and now, because in all these ways Robin and I had a perfect understanding.

When he went from this world, he left his own finances in a state of chaos. Of course, he did not expect to hear at fifty-five that he would be dead in nine months from cancer, but I do not think it would have made a damn of difference if he had, and I was with him all the way. I shall always think that he was right, and so I turned from the window that evening, turned from the life we had made, unrepentant, but broke. I glanced at the room as I walked through it, where, with the aid, no doubt, of a large expense account, we had enjoyed playing host to the greats of the artistic world of our day.

When Robin died, he was Chairman in England of the International Famous Agency, but he and his company had recently been sold lock, stock and barrel to Americans who now owned him as well as the rest of the organization. When the news broke that he was not too well, they started moving the furniture out of his office. 'Fox is on the skids.' He certainly was. I received on his death a typed letter of condolence from the United States. I still have the letter in my files.

Robin had a very big salary and I expect there was some capital accruing from an American deal, but he never discussed money with me. The agency paid for Eaton Square and the lavish way we entertained there. Of course, a lot of perks were ours, which included travelling all over the world first class and having a car and chauffeur at our disposal.

All this stopped like a clock the day he died. Looking back does no good, but I have to laugh at myself for being so spoilt in the material sense and for taking it as a right, as a matter of course. Robin's salary ceased and there was no pension, just a curt letter, also in my files, to this effect. There was no compensation of any sort, but, above all, no thanks to him for the business he had made for them and the work that he had created for a lot of lesser people than himself.

It took ten years to learn from an evening paper that Robin Fox's estate was nil and this came about because solicitors and accountants had been instructed by Robin's Sole Executor to take me on. There had, in fact, been a large enough sum to provide for the Foxes for another ten years. In the middle of the proceedings, the accountant actually disappeared, taking all his information concerning the estate with him. He may have taken a good deal more besides, but I had no means at my disposal of following this up.

I gave up writing to what was termed 'my solicitor' for clarification so that I might try to cut my coat according to the cloth. When I realized what he charged to write a note in reply, saying, 'Yours of the 1st inst. received, Yours faithfully', I knew even a vast fortune would not last long.

It must have cost a great deal to visit the solicitor to try to explain that I thought it very foolish for me to keep on a flat in Eaton Square, although that will have cost very little compared to prices today. The visit added considerably to the rent. He would take half an hour to tell me in soothing terms that there was no reason why this should not be paid out of the estate, as I was used to such luxury. I see now that it was easier just to fool me while they messed about, and kept me quiet while they watched their own interests. I got some cash for food and clothes by letting the flat during the summer to a tax-exile Earl, but finally I pulled myself together and went, as I should have done before, to my son's father-in-law, Harry Sporborg.

I sought his advice and I took it, and within three months the firm to which he had sent me clarified the position, explained why I had nothing, and asked if I would like to report the solicitors who had been looking after me to the Law Society. Realizing I could never afford to do this and that all I wanted to do was to forget the whole thing, I declined.

I came to terms with it quite quickly when they explained why I had nothing, but, of course, in relation to other people's misfortunes, 'nothing' was not quite the case. I had two houses I could sell to raise money to live on, one in Sussex and one in Cornwall, and I owned this cottage where I am now. I was very, very lucky, and so away I went from Eaton Square, but I admit if ever I am in a strange solicitor's office again, unless the senior partners are my friends, I shall have been taken there screaming and in chains.

7

Pebbles on the Beach

After Robin's death I lost, through illness or accident, so many friends so quickly that I know about the depth of despair. Shakespeare said, 'Troubles never singly come, but in battalions', and he knew a thing or two.

My worst surprise of all was when Cocky Farr telephoned me and asked, 'What are you doing, Angela?' It was a hot summer's day. I was packing rather more carefully than usual because I was going for the weekend to stay with my friend, Godfrey Winn, at his house in Falmer, near Lewes.

'I am packing. Godfrey has got one of his tennis weekends and he has invited me to play hostess.'

'You will not be doing that – Godfrey is dead.'

So long had our friendship been, so strange, so fraught with difficulties, so very very close, that it still pains me to write that last sentence. We met in 1937 at a weekend party at the house near Wallingford of our American millionaire friend, Howard Jay Gould. I was pregnant with Edward and, on getting up rather late one morning after a luxurious breakfast in bed, I went downstairs, wandered through the house on my way to watch whatever sport was being played by the rest of the house party. *En route* to the garden, I went into the sun lounge to read the newspapers, where a fair young man with a good-looking baby face was sprawled on a sofa. He rose to greet me. 'I am Godfrey Winn.' We shook hands and a friendship started that many people tried to end and that only concluded with his violent, unexpected death in 1973.

Very shortly before he died, he had published what was to be his last book. He gave a party for all the booksellers in Southern England. I think he and Daphne du Maurier and Somerset Maugham were the highest-paid writers in the land. He understood public relations as no one else did until Jeffrey Archer came on the scene. He had a genius for selling the goods he had prepared so carefully and, although he was the best-known journalist in the land, I always teased him and called him 'The Birmingham Businessman'. He enjoyed that, because it was, in fact, the background he had come from.

Godfrey had arranged the seating for his book-launching dinner party with his usual care, and I was put between Asa Briggs, then Vice-Chancellor of Sussex University, and a well-known doctor with a particular knowledge and understanding of cancer, the radiologist Dr Jan de Winter. These men knew Godfrey very well and both said true things about him to me that evening. The second one I should have heeded more carefully, and then perhaps my own doctor's stark announcement would not have floored me, and literally thousands of others, as it did. What Asa Briggs said was that Godfrey was the best-known, highest-paid – probably ever

– journalist, a household name like the television personalities of today, but that if he died suddenly, all this would be forgotten in a day. Asa's words came true very quickly.

Godfrey rose to his feet to make a short, well-prepared speech. I had witnessed this scene so many times. He jumped up, so vital, so alive, so enjoying being the absolute centre of attention – something he was used to, but it still gave him a kick. He earned the applause that followed his brief, to-the-point words, by never letting up on intense hard work and self-discipline.

A long time had passed since we had first met and now he was an older, balding, baby-faced man, still buoyant, but the years were telling. He was, as always, impeccably well turned out and, to my eye (which I now see as very untrained) fit and well. I suppose I was so used to him that I accepted without thinking that my very dear, but very vain, friend thought almost continually of the impression he was creating, and this had to be of a fit, strong, athletic type, whom age would never touch . . .

And so when Dr Jan de Winter, who played hard games of tennis with him several times a week, told me that he was worried about him and had had to warn him several times that he must take life much more easily or the consequences could be serious, I took no notice of his words. Foolish of me, as Cocky Farr, who had examined him, repeatedly said the same thing. But within months Godfrey was dead and, in as little time, forgotten.

So both men were right.

*

There were many sides to Godfrey. He could be bewildering, and each of his intimate friends would give a different account of what he did or said. One thing they all knew for certain; each man and woman would, and still will, assure you that he or she was his very best friend, that he or she was the only one he loved and turned to, the only one in whom he confided. This is what he told us all and we believed him. He made us feel good and needed. He dedicated his books rapturously to all of us, and to none more than to me and my family.

He was homosexual, but very discreet. I knew only two of his lovers. He kept his many lives secret and apart from one another. One lover was a dancer-designer, whom he adored, and who nearly destroyed him when he left him to get married. The other was an older man, whom Robin and I had known and liked long before we knew Godfrey. He was a sophisticated, rather witty, quiet man and a good influence in a worldly way on many eminent people, known and trusted even in Royal circles. Robin and I just thought of these two as good friends.

Peter, the older one, was rather a stabilizing influence on violent, intense Godfrey, and they often went away together on what they said would be a quiet holiday. Robin actually detested Godfrey, but was fond of Peter. It was shortly after Robin died that I remember Godfrey and Peter setting off for Rome to enjoy a few days' respite from their busy lives. I was surprised when, a day or two after their return, Godfrey telephoned. He must come over, he needed my help desperately. Surprised, as it was around midnight, but fairly used to hysterical outbursts, I stopped my preparations for bed, got myself dressed and put on a proper make-up, or Godfrey would have made unflattering remarks. I need not have bothered. When he arrived, he was distraught, completely hysterical. Peter had thrown himself under a train.

I remember thinking I must play this very quietly. I set about rekindling the nursery fire and sat him in a deep armchair, and went and made a large jug of Ovaltine and told him to tell me, if he wished, what had happened.

It appeared that, when they were in Rome, Godfrey had indulged rather indiscreetly in a foolish liaison with a young waiter from the restaurant where they had eaten every day. I had never realized the depth of Peter's feelings before this. I was now told how he had been pained so often that he was almost always miserably jealous. I sat thinking how little we knew of each other. Just as well, probably. I was sad for Peter's suffering, but detached about their relationship. I considered it then, as I do now, interesting in a way, but surprising, and absolutely none of my business.

Godfrey's mother was, I felt, responsible for many of his problems. She was a tough, pretty woman, an excellent gardener, a talent she passed on to this gifted son of hers, who spent a fortune on plants for her. But she had loved her other son, Roger, more. As a child Roger had been a victim of infantile paralysis and, left with a very pronounced limp, had been given all of the mother's love. He became a brilliant and respected judge – more of an intellectual and very different from Godfrey. For a civilian, he rose to great heights during the Second World War and served at the Admiralty. I never once saw him at Godfrey's, never heard from Godfrey that Roger had been to visit their mother.

Godfrey lavished his time, his care, his life on his mother. He paid for her to have lovely homes and whatever holidays she announced she had a fancy for, and he kept giving parties in her honour. She dressed expensively – a tough, egocentric woman. And she was what I always find very dangerous and difficult to deal with – 'a sweet woman'.

Godfrey told me he took her to a party given in his honour by Sir Archibald McIndoe at the Queen Victoria Hospital in East Grinstead. 'Archie' saw the best in Godfrey, as he did in all of us, and he would make the best sides come true. Godfrey had endured agonizing fear in war, but as a reporter had flown on many sorties and been the champion and friend of the men he flew with. These mutilated, very young men, who were given new faces by Archie, became known, as they are today, as the 'Guinea Pigs'.

In a speech that night Archie gave sincere praise to Godfrey for his courage and for the example he had set, and, when the time came to go home and he was carefully settling his mother in the car to drive her home, she said, 'At last. This is the first time in your life that I have not been ashamed of you.'

For that I hated her. This son was not loved, so he developed into a tough, resilient survivor. He overcame a timid nature, longing to be loved. He was vain, but took an interest in everyone he met, observed them and helped people in all walks of life to make the best of themselves. He was courteous, but even more famous for being mean, and yet he was the only man who ever gave me money, unasked, when I was in trouble. When the war broke out, only Godfrey Winn, of all my friends, asked how I was going to manage and provide for my family. Robin's family could have helped but didn't. My own family would have, but could not.

I learned, when he had gone, that Jan de Winter and Cocky Farr had told him bluntly that his heart had had its day. He must stop playing tennis or he would die on the court. Godfrey promptly arranged a tennis tournament for the next weekend. In the meantime he would practise because he always had to win. He had played at Wimbledon as a boy and was still pretty good. So he asked a young friend, a fine player, to join him, to put in some good work before the other guests arrived. They had some fast sets and the young man was worn out and said he must stop, Godfrey was killing him.

'Come on, one more set,' insisted Godfrey.

But it was himself that he was killing. He threw up the ball to serve an ace and smashed it, and smashed on the ground the face he had taken such care of all his life. He fell dead with such force that, when they picked him up, there was no longer any face left.

I learned this from Lord Rupert Nevill, who used these words and who, as was typical of him, went at once to see if he could be of any help to Godfrey's staff and friends. He heard of this awful event before anyone else because he and Godfrey shared a secretary, Mrs Cumberland-Brown. 'Brownie' loved them both equally, and she was right to. They were both wonderful people.

It was Rupert Nevill who finished off something Godfrey had always tried to teach me. One night I was with the Nevills and Rupert said he wanted to talk to me, and talk he did – the three of us sitting by a big log fire. His wife Mickey was doing a tapestry and scarcely spoke. He had a large cardboard box beside him, and he showed me and told me about the contents of this box. It was not Pandora's, but it was Rupert Nevill's – full of letters, obituaries, poems, even drawings, all records of relatives and friends of his who, like Robin, had died. He told me sometimes sad, sometimes funny, always moving stories of many of them, some old, some his contemporaries, some very young, and without sentimentality but with true feeling, of all they meant to him. I shall never, never forget so much he told me – when, finally standing by my bedroom door, we said good night. After thanking him, I asked, 'Why did you take all this trouble?'

He replied, 'You simply had to learn to accept that none of us is the only pebble on the beach.' I hope he and Godfrey knew what important pebbles they were to me.

Rupert's work was Secretary and Treasurer to the Duke of Edinburgh, and his office was at Buckingham Palace; he was one of the busiest men I have ever known. But when Robin came back from the Issels Clinic in Germany and he had very little time left in this world, Rupert would often break his journey to and from London to stop off at our house and just sit with Robin, who was unconscious, and hold his hand. He always brought strength and comfort to me. He was at Robin's funeral and thereafter he and Mickey were friends for whom I thank God every day.

It was not so long after Godfrey's death that Rupert died himself. I miss him for one rather curious reason; he never made anything very easy for me. For instance I recall him telephoning one evening and saying that he and Mickey were suddenly and quite unexpectedly alone – something very unusual for them – and that I must drive over and have dinner with them and stay the night.

'I can't. I can't drive myself any more.'

'What nonsense. Get in the car. We shall expect you in an hour.'

Down went the receiver. The night was wicked, the snow was falling fast. The car skidded all over the place. I was in utter panic. I spotted a telephone box at the side of the road, staggered from my car to ring the Nevills' number.

'I am stuck on a steep hill. I can't go on.'

'Absolute nonsense. We are keeping dinner waiting for you. You can.'

He was right. I could. We can all manage the impossible if the Rupert Nevills of this world tell us we can.

Godfrey had come to lunch with me in the country exactly a week before he died. His mood was ebullient. He had just returned from a tour of the United States. Success had ridden with him all the way, so he was dressed as a cowboy. This was a considerable relief, for one was never sure which mood, which love or hate, he would bring with him. It was one of those days when his theme was, 'I'm going to leave you all my money, Angie, all my furniture, all my pictures, everything I possess.' In fact, rumour has it – I think correctly – that he left everything that really mattered to his niece, his brother's daughter. They had never been very close, but Godfrey had the conventional, family man side to him, and he was very shrewd about money. He never resented it when I teased him on that score. All his references to money were just jokes that we had shared over the years, never to be taken seriously. It was a sort of party piece. There may have been friends who were interested in him because of his worldly success – the fortune he had built up, and the beautiful furniture and pictures that he had acquired by his own efforts – but he knew as well as I did that our friendship was not based on anything as devious as that. We were quite simply devoted to each other. He is someone I miss all the time, his bad moods as well as his good ones – most of all, the fun and the laughter that we shared.

One of the best things that he did leave me was a most unlikely friendship that I am still enjoying with someone who was probably more important to him than anyone else. This was Joanna Kelly, who had been Governor of Holloway Prison for fourteen years. I think he met her when he went to interview her.

She is an intellectual and deeply spiritual woman, so I spend a lot of time wondering what it is that makes me fortunate enough to enjoy her friendship. She is also very much a woman of the world. She is extremely discreet and never misses one trick in the book, which can terrify the lights out of me.

Soon after Robin died, Godfrey asked me, 'Is there anything in particular you need, Angie?' 'Yes, to meet Joanna Kelly again.' He arranged this when she was staying a weekend with him at his house in Falmer. We walked together in Stanmer Park woods, kicking the leaves on this winter's day – just Joanna and I. Godfrey went indoors to do some work. We walked slowly for nearly an hour in complete silence, only broken when she said, looking at her watch, 'Time to go in for lunch.' Joanna's silence was – and is – more important than all the well-meant words of sympathy and advice that pour from most good friends. She gave me strength.

8

The Smart Life

Through all the changes of role I adopted, I still entertained the idiotic idea that going away, going abroad preferably, would help me come face to face with myself, whoever that stranger might be.

One dark January George and Patricia Harewood invited me to stay with them in Barbados. 'Vice', they always called me, because I had remained Vice-Chairman of the ENO Benevolent Fund under George, then Jennie Lee, then Patricia. An uncle of mine, to whom I had never been very kind, did me a wonderful service just at that moment. He died unexpectedly and left me enough money to set out on this unlikely holiday; I was thrilled at the thought of doing something so different and, having once been so daring, went three years running.

The first year George rented a very grand villa. In the material sense it was paradise, a beautiful house, with wonderful servants, headed by Joseph, the best butler on the island. We were waited on hand and foot, and, for three weeks, did nothing but swim, sunbathe and sleep. The sea lapped the garden wall.

Occasionally in the evenings we went inland, or rather to the other side of the island, to visit planter friends of George in their colonial-style houses. George knew some owners of sugar plantations, as the Harewoods had been very big land-owners themselves in Barbados, and were still considered an important family there. These islanders were kind hosts to us and we would stand around for hours on hot evenings drinking wonderful rum punches before dinner was finally served. We would hear not so much about the island and what was happening there – this would have been stimulating, as they were facing many labour problems at the time – but more about the flats that they owned in Knightsbridge, how often they came to England, and what they thought of Harrods and the English theatre.

So we were always glad to come back to our house near the beach and go to bed and lie listening to the cicadas and the sound of the sea washing the shore, getting it ready for the trippers from England, Canada and America, who would lie around the next day. We had about one hundred yards of beach to ourselves and George and Patricia would lie on the white sand in the blazing sun. I always chose the shade of the palm trees on the edge of the shore, knowing that tomorrow and tomorrow and tomorrow we need do nothing but lead this idle life, swimming, reading, eating and sleeping. Such a blissful time.

Our villa was in the St James's area of the island. Grumbling a bit, we did accept just two local invitations. One was to take tea, something I wanted to do more than anybody else, with Oliver Messel, who died not long after this first trip to the island. He lived in a house that he had created himself – and in his heyday he had been responsible for many other beautiful houses on the island. I remembered him as the most gifted of theatre designers: Robin and I had had most to do with him when he designed the set for *The Little Hut*, which starred Robert Morley, and it was from the proceeds of our small investment in this production that we sent Edward and James to Harrow. I felt sentimentally grateful to Oliver Messel, whose work contributed greatly to this success, as it did to everything he undertook.

Now, however, he had come to the end of the road. He was quite alone – even without servants, it seemed – in the loveliest house I suppose I shall ever visit, so much in harmony with the sea and the beach and the palm trees surrounding it that it was very difficult to know, because of the way he had used mirrors, whether you were indoors or out in his garden.

What a sad little tea party it turned out to be, rather as if we had been visiting a nanny who had run out of money; I think I saw a brown teapot and just one rather stale sponge cake, but no other visitors. Oliver's friend and lifelong companion had recently died.

I noticed a large tapestry lying unfinished in the hall. George observed my eye stray towards it and said, 'Don't say anything, that is the work Varne was doing when he died.'

During tea we naturally talked only of the past. For this great designer there was no future and he had, apparently, fallen out with a great many of the jet-set society who frequented the island simply for holidays. Oliver kept jumping up and rushing to a garden door, taking pieces of the sponge cake with him.

'What are you doing, Oliver?' I asked him.

'Oh don't say anything, I am feeding the monkeys. We are forbidden to encourage them, but they are the only friends I have left.'

Of course none of us ever saw him again; he died shortly after that sad tea party. I think that what he brought to our theatre was quite irreplaceable.

The other house we visited was next door. It belonged to Eileen Maremont, who had married an American millionaire, having previously been the wife of Larry Adler, the harmonica player. During her time as Mrs Adler I had known her slightly in England. I think the house had been designed by Oliver: he had used the natural setting, making the house seem like an Aladdin's cave built on the rocks above a small private bay.

We walked through this enchanted castle out on to the terrace for drinks in the moonlight, the stars so bright that looking up through the trees one thought hospitable, rich Eileen had been shopping for fairy lights. Even at dinner time it was too hot to wear anything but the thinnest cotton evening dress, and I do not think that I wore shoes. There was no artificial light on the terrace where we met our fellow guests – quite a lot of them were interesting Bajans, politicians, lawyers and doctors, living and working on the island.

We then dined out of doors by candlelight, where their dark skins made it difficult to have a very clear picture of them. But the personalities were strong, their charm and intelligence formidable. Our party was glad that it had made the effort to accept such delightful and unusual hospitality.

Each time I returned to England in February to find it

wet, grey, cold, murky and miserable, I thought, 'Why the hell do I live here?' I had the answer: I liked it! But I would be a bigger liar than usual if I said I did not plan, as I landed at Heathrow, to save up for twelve months, so that next January I could fulfil my desire to turn round and go back to that white sand and those palm trees.

The following two years George rented houses that were just as nice but smaller. There was not quite so much super luxury, which was just as well as one's feet would never have got near the ground. We were joined by an American friend of theirs, Nancy Lasalle, who had a great interest in the New York City Ballet, and she and I would put on spurts of energy and cross to Atlantic Bay on the other side of the island and watch the native boys surfing on huge waves.

Nancy and I would take a picnic and sit for hours on the beach watching them, like two children unable to believe their eyes. On the return journey, I always enjoyed the intense games of cricket that were going on in every village street as we drove through, very serious games in the heat and the dust. I used to wonder which one of the players we would shortly see hitting our English team for six at Lord's.

On our last visit, we went via New York and we travelled on Concorde. I was as excited as a child when George took us to the Metropolitan Opera House to hear Pavarotti sing in *Un Ballo in Maschera*. I stayed with Nancy Lasalle, but I also wanted to see Ronda, my old friend, who had been so good to me. She had an apartment near Nancy on Fifth Avenue.

We returned home by Concorde, but hanging about waiting for it took nearly a day. At Kennedy Airport we were treated like spoiled VIPs, apologized to and given caviar to keep us quiet. It was only after a short journey, but after many hours of waiting to take it, that on landing in England we caught up with reality and were denied the privileges we had so quickly taken for granted.

Brusque rudeness at every level was the order of the day – there were no porters, and we were shoved in every direction. George was such an experienced traveller that this held no surprises for him. But even he showed slight irritation when, having got two trolleys for our luggage, he was pulling our heavy cases on to one of them and the second trolley was whisked from under our noses by a fellow passenger whom Patricia and I had been too slow to stop. That was the trolley that broke the Earl's temper – after twenty-four hours spent getting from New York using the fastest aircraft on earth.

How did I pay the Concorde fare? It seems perfectly clear that I am always harassed about money, but if I have a fancy to do something, I will do it. Concorde, of course, is a thrill, but having done it and being able to say you have done it is rather like name-dropping – silly but quite fun.

The best part of these holidays in Barbados was the perfect friendship I shared with George and Patricia. Never one second were we out of harmony. Every moment was pleasant, even the hours we spent travelling. We were so happy there – beautiful Patricia, so athletic and such a fine swimmer, while George and I were rather nervous in the waves, inclined to stay nearer the beach and not dive through them as she did. Early every morning George and Patricia would go off for a long, long walk together over the miles of white sand before the heat hit it. It must have been good for them to escape from the hectic life that they led in England, where they gave so much time and attention to the English National Opera and fulfilled all the commitments that they had in Yorkshire. They used to go by train from London to Leeds and so to Harewood House nearly every weekend and, even there, seldom had a moment alone. Barbados was the place where all three of us were lucky enough to recharge our energies in order to return and face whatever problems turned up.

I think they had much more energy than I had, because when they asked me to go to India, I regret I did not accept. The visit was to include much sight-seeing and meeting of Indian friends whom they had known for many years, attending performances of Indian dancing and listening to Indian music. I was not ready. This may sound feeble, but I feared I might let them down. The visit would have incurred flying in small aeroplanes to many different states, and I had a memory of a flight in the West Indies when one day George said we must all go to Martinique and we were packed like sardines into a very small aeroplane. I had hated that flight so much that I felt I would be a dead loss if asked to do this all over India. I wanted instead to leave them with good memories of their holiday companion.

Quite another side of the coin of my mania to escape got me as far as the Engadine in Switzerland. I had a distinguished friend in the world of pictures. Her name was Lilian Browse. I had met her when Robin was alive and she had helped him very much with an exhibition of the works of Rodin when, rather against his will, Robin had undertaken to run the Sussex Festival. We became very good friends.

She owned an interesting gallery, Roland Browse and Delbanco, in Cork Street, and, when we bought pictures, we did it through her. We bought what we wanted, but her advice was invaluable. If George Harewood taught me to listen to music, Lilian taught me how to look at pictures.

She was married to a businessman called Sydney Lines and, in 1980, the three of us flew to Zurich where we picked up a car and made for the Engadine. They knew of a small, clean, adequate hotel where we stayed. I hated every moment. All the trees we were supposed to enjoy looking at had a disease. They were either dead or dying, and it made me feel nervous and sad. Every morning I awoke shaking and literally praying for help to get me through the day and not let them see how desperate – in fact ill with misery – I felt.

Why are we all so ashamed to confess mental pain? After the ordeal and agony of Robin's slow death, I used to break my ankle, sprain my wrist, or get a slipped disc, and I received sympathy and was noticed. But when I felt nervously distraught, I could not give way to it because I knew I should be looked upon as a highly undisciplined woman, wishing to call attention to herself, and I knew the advice would be, 'Pull yourself together.' Oh, how I wanted to do just that.

'Oh, God,' I kept saying, as I shook and shook with tears pouring down my face. 'Oh, God, just help me, help me to pull myself together.' I knew then, and I know now, I was just one of many millions shaking in despair, in fear of inexplicable fear. If ever I had let anyone see me in that state, I should have been accused of self-pity, and the accuser would have been absolutely right. I was, however, terrified that anyone should see the miserable wreck that I was. What would have happened, I wonder, if I had gone to my travelling companions and said, 'I do apologize, but I am standing on a precipice and I am about to fall into a bottomless pit. I know it is inconsiderate, but I am having a nervous breakdown.'

I shall never know because I could not pull myself together enough to say it and I have just, only just, managed to control the impulse. But I have read enough, listened enough, ever since that visit to Switzerland to know my plight was a very common one.

My mother, Glitters, rose above so many problems. I remember as always she was interested and amused, but if ever we thought to say, 'How are you?' she would reply cheerfully, 'Cold, sick, tired, frightened and hungry.' Well that is about it. She could have added, 'Lonely' . . . but that would have been going too far.

There were excursions all over Switzerland, and some days we felt really adventurous and would go over the border into Italy. But the day which stays most firmly in my mind is the one when we went to Austria.

We bought our bread, cheese, fruit and wine, which was the lunchtime menu for these jaunts. We must have gone through Customs, but all I recall is being in a meadow, full of wild flowers, looking down on a valley, with mountains in the distance. I seem to think we heard birds singing, because it crossed my mind that there would have been shots assaulting our ears if the day had been Sunday.

It was an idyllic scene and, after the picnic had gone down the red lane, my companions fell into a deep sleep – something I usually did as well, which proved that there wasn't anything much the matter with me except exhaustion, which I was always refusing to admit.

This day I did not sleep. Emotions got the upper hand again, because, although what met my eyes was like a painting by Monet – peasants working in the field below, piling hay on to wagons drawn by horses, a picture of perfect peace – all I had in my mind was my last, very different, visit to Austria. The time I remembered was when I was invited by friends who lived in Kitzbühel to take a day off from watching my husband dying in the clinic near Munich. How I had looked forward to this break! But I was then in the grip of such agonizing emotions caused by having to watch my friend, my companion of thirty-seven years, dying while undergoing the appalling treatments he was subjected to at the infamous Issels Clinic, that I was incapable of enjoying the warmth and kindness extended to me. Quite irrationally, I have hated this part of the world, despite its beauty, ever since.

I realize, after eighteen years, that the wounds we all receive will heal, if we let them. I would like to go to Austria again and picnic in the summer in the fields and watch my grandchildren skiing in the winter.

I am often considered lucky to have travelled all over the world, to have met so many interesting people, to have known extreme luxury at the Ritz in Paris, the Carlton at Cannes in the old days, and suchlike treats. But, if I look back truthfully my memory of greatest enjoyment and happiness is of standing on a May day in an uncultivated patch of ground at Epple Bay Cottage, just outside Birchington, where we lived. My mother had acquired this bolt hole as somewhere that we could all escape to and enjoy, and, although it was so near our home, it was always an adventure to go there.

The moment in childhood I liked best was standing on this May day in the rough grass near the cottage door with Polly and Lizzie, our Nanny's sisters. Lizzie said, 'Listen, there's a lark. Look up there, look, there it is.' We looked up and saw the lark and remained quiet together for quite a time. The peace and tranquillity of that moment, with those two dear, simple friends, has never been matched by any of my so-called glamorous adventures.

I had an equally memorable day on my twenty-first birthday. It is quite the happiest memory I have of my mother. We were in a garden just as undisciplined as the Birchington one which went with a house called Pardons in Ditchling, Sussex. We found some rugs and broken-down deck chairs and had a picnic, just like the one all those years later in Austria. But my twenty-first birthday was carefree, full of family gossip and laughter, in simple surroundings. I have to laugh at myself now and wonder why I spend so much of my time making houses tidy and cultivating the garden.

I was a poor companion to my friends on their Swiss holiday. I remember waking every morning thinking, 'I cannot face today . . . I cannot face car driving and sight-seeing.' I hung on, overcoming inexplicable panic. When we returned to our hotel in Zurich, we planned a pleasant evening dining in a slightly more sophisticated way before catching the aeroplane home. I upset the apple-cart by clumsily tripping on a step near my bedroom door and breaking my ankle. I feel sure that every accident that befalls us is caused by an inability to cope with some situation we cannot resolve, and it also seems that we are most of us too proud to confess this feeling to other people, thereby denying ourselves the chance to sort out the problem. I am convinced that that was why I had this accident. I blame it on stress. My ankle was broken and so I had to slow down and start recovering from the muddle I was in. So for me, in one way at least, this holiday paid off.

PART THREE

9

The Visitors

When Jennie Lee retired from the ENO Benevolent Fund she had chaired so well, she took me to lunch at the House of Lords, and during lunch asked me if I knew of a cottage in the country she could rent. 'Of course,' said I, 'the one in my garden.' The deal was done there and then and I asked her for ten pounds a week. I had not yet become a business woman. Jennie was my tenant for two years. She said she wanted the cottage for her nephew, Vincent Stafford, and his then wife Gisella, who was also at lunch, and she said she would live there with them as she wanted so much to see more of them and to get to know their children, whom she looked upon as her grandchildren.

I made another essay into voluntary work and this kept me from Cuckfield when they first moved into Buntings, which has now become my home. When I did get to Ockenden Cottage, they were firmly in residence and a fairly difficult and rather sad state of affairs appeared to be brewing.

This was in great contrast to my weekday life in London,

where there were still a lot of laughs to be had, some of them caused by mistakes I made of always wanting to mix the 'gentry' and the theatre, although I was forever giving lectures to my children about how separate our worlds were. I remember one evening particularly. I don't know what possessed me, but I had invited a charming lady I hardly knew, called Lady Henriette Abel-Smith, and her husband, Sir Alex Abel-Smith, for dinner. Alec Guinness and Jill Bennett were other guests.

The evening was going fairly well, although not the best party I have ever given, when Robert Morley burst in like a tornado, as was his way, and flung himself on the sofa next to Sir Alex, who, not knowing whom he was taking on, immediately tackled Robert on his more recent plays and expressed dislike for his work generally. Unlike any other type of man, Robert was delighted by this sort of behaviour – it was as if he had had a tonic.

'Ah,' he said, 'I know who you are, you're a banker, one of those fellows who cause all the trouble in the world, and Angela says you are a Master of Hounds. I bet she has made that up, she always exaggerates, but I'm sure you ride horses, and if you're not careful, I shall tell you which way you ought to face when you get on the animal's back.'

And so, of course, the evening died a death. I got the giggles like a schoolgirl. Lady Henriette behaved impeccably, but I could see by her face that she was wondering what she was doing with these extraordinary people, and they hastily bade their adieux and vanished. I made yet another vow not to invite people to my house unless I could guarantee them a happy evening.

Alec Guinness had remained absolutely dignified and well

behaved and not uttered one word. But when we repaired to the kitchen, as we always did, to see if Betty needed a final hand with the washing up, he did an impression of the proceedings which covered all the characters who had been at dinner. It became one of those occasions when I knew we were all going to die laughing – and we would not have minded a bit. Where Alec is such a genius is that he managed this without for one second being unkind. How he made us laugh!

If ever I could explain Alec Guinness I should, indeed, be clever. I find it quite impossible. As a companion he can be the wickedest, wittiest, most observant, wise and even most spiritual man that I have ever met. I might try to fool some of the people some of the time. This is not an exercise I would ever embark on with Alec Guinness.

When I returned to spend the summer in Cuckfield, the fun was fast and furious. The young Staffords had taken over, and Jennie, whose idea the whole thing had been, was on the wrong end of the stick. I felt sorry for her, but it was quite understandable. They would all arrive from London on Fridays for their country weekend, Jennie to be quiet and get on with her book about her husband, Aneurin Bevan, and the young ones to enjoy themselves and cram as many of their friends as they could into the cottage to enjoy fun in the country.

Vincent was a television producer, an attractive if rather vague young man, and very much the spoilt, indulged nephew of Jennie. I saw him as the son she without doubt wished she had had, and he was used to getting his own way on every count. He had his lovely wife, Gisella, and two pretty angels they assured me were their daughters.

Robert and Celestia and their first child, Chlöe, came to stay nearly every weekend with me and an immediate firm friendship was formed with the Staffords; and so now from Friday to Sunday night Jennie and I were overrun by hordes of young men and women and their children, and we would wander together in my part of the garden telling each other how happy we were. We were lying. She was even older than me and a little too fat, but never can there have been such a peaches and cream complexion or such magnificent snow-white hair. She had crafty brown eyes that shone full of wickedness like a naughty child's – an immensely bright and brainy star who found it real hell not to be the centre of attention.

I found Jennie's courage rather touching. In fact, rather like me, she was trying to create a new world to live in because the door had slammed on the one she had inhabited when her husband, Aneurin Bevan, left the room – when he died.

As I knew nothing about politics, which had been her whole life, I probably saw her differently from most people. I certainly feel that she missed her husband every hour, every second, of her life. I never knew him, but I was introduced to him and we spoke briefly during the interval of a play at the Phoenix Theatre. The meeting was only a moment, but I shall never forget him; so strong was his magnetic personality that I felt that I knew him well and I still do, it is quite uncanny.

Now Jennie had spent a life in politics, which was their joint concern, with this fascinating, rebellious Welshman, and listening to her through the long summer which she spent writing a book about him, I learned of the rage and turbulent furies that they often felt in their private life, but I was always aware of the passion that held them together before, during and after all these storms. Living as I do in the world of entertainment, I think the story of these two people and the contribution that they made to the lives of many whom they cared about would make a great television series, more dramatic than idiotic *Dallas*, stimulating and instructive about the social and political history of the time, and above all it would be about a love affair ... But where are the stars big enough to give us even a glimpse of these two characters who were so much larger than life?

Jennie and I found something in common, I believe, in our immense sense of relief on Sunday nights when, with the engines of smart cars revving up and voices screaming above the noise making arrangements for the next weekend and children bellowing, the cars would be put into gear and move off much too fast out of the courtyard that separated our two houses. Vincent and Gisella took away a dream of Jennie Lee's with them; she had thought she was going to spend quiet weekends learning to know better her beloved nephew and his wife and the two lovely little girls. They were to be her family, her children and her grandchildren. Only someone who has never had children of her own could ever have entertained such a pipe dream. When Vincent and Gisella were here, it was, in fact, the end of their own violent love affair, the end of their marriage and the short years of stability that their children had known.

Jennie was hurt and disturbed and minded deeply for the children, and, quite naturally, a bit for herself as well. She was so used to getting her own way, or at least to thinking that she was getting it. I could not alter anything for her, but would play my cynical performance, one I had played so often, of being truthful. I had acted it many weekends on exactly the same set with Robin, but oddly enough we had stayed together. I know that to Jennie the mood was not unknown, but she took no heed and she chose not to remember that she had been as violent and as selfish as her young ones – as we all are when we are growing up.

The marriage ended with the second autumn that they were here. When it was hot and my bedroom windows were open, I could hear their agonizing rows. It was like listening to *Rigoletto*. They came over to Ockenden Cottage often and talked with me, both claiming to be glad that their relationship was finished. It is only now when I run into them by accident, probably in a theatre where Robert has a play, that I find they both look back on those days as having the Colour of the Rose.

When they had departed on Sunday evenings, I would join Jennie for a quiet drink. Like many lonely people she drank a little too much – probably managing a few more drinks than me. I never had a good head so I always went home before I sounded silly, something that she could never be. If the weather was good, she would decide to stay the week at the cottage and continue with writing her book about Nye.

I would go back home and start clearing up the ravages of the weekend, have some supper and go to bed. Jennie, I think, worked on, kept herself awake for as long as she wished, probably managing this by drinking more than ever I could. Undaunted, as always, she would appear at my kitchen door early next morning to have coffee with me. I certainly could have done without her in the early hours, but I had to laugh because the part she was playing, that of the eminent political authoress, caused her to be most oddly dressed. She always appeared wearing an old-fashioned black bathing dress. As far as I know, she had never been near the sea or a pool. And very, very shabby, immensely high-heeled white sandals that had seen better days.

After coffee, she would totter back across the courtyard to her lonely writing and in the evenings we would meet again and talk. It was no good asking her to a meal as she ate less than anyone I have ever met. She talked, of course, of the past. She touched on famous names in her political world, but with me, anyway, she never descended to gossip. The person who was most important to her in her day-to-day life was Lord Goodman. No moves were made, no views were held that were not dominated by the advice of Arnold. Ever since our ENO days, he and I would see each other occasionally at a dinner or lunch party, but we never managed to be anything but very guarded and almost hostile to each other. But I know for a fact through close mutual friends that a kinder, more caring man to his friends than this brilliant lawyer has never lived. I have to try not to be rather irked by my failure to get his attention, particularly as I hear Robin's voice whenever I see him: 'Arnold Goodman – the cleverest of them all.' There was a side of Robin that enjoyed the law, and clever lawyers most of all, though he would swear this was not so. I would jump on my favourite hobby-horse: 'The one person we never know is ourselves – such a pity.'

Quite soon Jennie realized that country cottage life, no

matter how much it had suited her when Nye was alive, was no longer her cup of tea. When the two years were up she returned to her house in Chester Row.

*

When Jennie Lee and her brood finally decided the weekend cottage in the country was not for them, I did not want to see it empty for all the obvious reasons. The need to make some money on the side became ever more urgent. Through Asa and Susan Briggs, I met people who told me that it would be possible to let my cottage to academics who would be visiting Sussex University. I saw that this could be a good idea, as I would be paid but not have to become personally involved. Looking back, it is clear I had a somewhat hazy picture of visiting academics. An officious gentleman, who dealt with this problem for the university, called on me. He made rather a patronizing inspection of Buntings, but said he thought it quite suitable and was about to shake hands and depart, when I made what was probably the first mistake in this new venture. I pressed him to take tea with me at my house across the courtyard. He accepted and over the cups and buttered scones his whole attitude to me and the accommodation I had to offer changed perceptibly. I was treated to effusive praise of my wonderful taste and my beautiful home, etc., and I did realize, didn't I, that he would go to any lengths to find me the right tenant?

In finding what he considered to be this right person, he took no time at all. But, alas, he did not make the picture quite clear. Perhaps, to be fair, he could claim there was a language difficulty. But he certainly set a new drama going that started in rage and tears, but ended many months later, fortunately, in friendship and smiles.

The telephone call from the university told me that a Greek professor of economics of great renown, named Constantine Vaitsos, wished to move into the accommodation I offered with a wife and small child, immediately. 'Just give the professor the keys, that is all we need you to do.' I refrained from telling them that the cottage must be aired and brushed and scrubbed and dusted, the cupboards inspected and made spotless, the linen checked and the beds made up and the gas and electricity reconnected – and we all know how wearying that can be. And there were countless other tasks to be done before I considered my cottage pleasantly habitable so that I could actually take money from them. Mary Carter and I rolled up our sleeves and tackled the job at a feverish pace, and finally the little note was left on the highly polished table in the little entrance hall: 'Here are the keys. I am at my house. Please let me know if there is the least thing that I can do for you.'

Within an hour Constantine Vaitsos took me up on this. There was a violent, ferocious banging at my back door – the door nearest the cottage he was about to rent. I opened it to be faced by a furious young Greek speaking perfect English. He shrieked, 'You have insulted me. How could my wife and child be expected to sleep for even one night in a house that size?'

'Where did you expect to sleep?'

'This house. This is naturally the house they rented for us.'

'You are wrong. This is my house . . . and if you do not like the cottage I suggest you go elsewhere.'

'Where?'

'Go to a hotel in Lewes, there are plenty of them. It is the town most convenient for the university, and the people there must find you something worthy of your needs.'

I gave the handsome young Greek a list of hotels and firmly closed the door on him and decided that, when I felt calmer in the morning and less exhausted from getting the cottage ready, I would telephone the gentleman who had taken tea with me and tell him to find me a more easily recognizable type of professor, not a clever Greek million-aire. I did something very unusual for me, I poured myself a strong whisky and soda, sank into a huge armchair and turned on the television – and then fell asleep.

I was so tired that ordinarily I would only have woken at breakfast time, but in the pitch darkness I was roused by the sound of banging and, for a moment, I thought that I was dreaming of the Greek encounter. When the banging went on, I realized it was for real. Constantine had left at 5 p.m. I remember thinking, 'Whisky at five – I ought to wait till six, but I'm not going to.' It was now, in fact, eight o'clock and the TV was belting out some noisy *Top of the Pops* programme. The pounding on the door was obviously being perpetrated by somebody who had gone berserk. I flung it open.

There stood my Greek acquaintance, one hand raised to thump the door yet again, the other hand behind his back. On seeing me he relaxed. He beamed, and on came the charm that I was to grow used to every time he wanted something.

'Beware of Greeks bearing gifts,' he said, flashing film-star teeth at me and, from behind his back, he extended his hand which was clasping an enormous bunch of yellow roses.

What a disarming fellow he was and, once he got his own way, what a nice one. He and his wife and little boy moved into Buntings. At first it was clear they were making the best of a bad job, but gradually a friendship was formed; they wanted to be independent, and so did I, and we respected this.

I know Constantine did a great deal of work whilst there. Economics, even the word, is a mystery to me, but I learned that, in that world, he commanded respect. I really came to know them through his wife, Nicky, a small, elegant girl who I now see must have been lonely and, at times, bored – that is if there was time, because I suspect that in Geneva, where they came from before living in Sussex, there would have been servants and a nanny for her obstreperous, spoilt three-year-old son. In England she had to do it all herself and Constantine, a workaholic, demanded high standards in every department. Not an easy run for her money, and yet I still had the impression of a very happy marriage.

With Jennie Lee's group, the noise drifting across no man's land – the courtyard separating the two houses – was of voices raised in quarrel and the revving up of fast cars. When the Vaitsos were in residence, the sounds were the music of Beethoven, Mozart and Schubert. Rather good news – harmony is the word, I think. Constantine's stint at Sussex University came to an end after about nine months and he went to take up another appointment in Paris.

Variety, I have heard, is the spice of life. Well the spice of the next let was not as digestible. An odd stranger was thrown up on the shores of Cuckfield High Street. How and why, I can never ascertain, but my hairdresser, due to success, left a tiny shop for larger premises. The shop he left was little bigger than a large cupboard with no, what is termed I think, proper sanitary arrangements. His place was taken by a long-legged, elderly, chain-smoking, ex-show girl type American. She had bales and bales of dressmaking material of all weights with her, hideous tweeds, very English, she thought, and gaudy, synthetic yards for evening 'gowns'. She was a sad, lonely woman living in a fantasy world. Cuckfield had become a suburb of London – or of Brighton or Horsham, which were nearer – and this was now where she thought clothes or materials for Rome dressmaking would be bought.

Dale – she said that was her name – put in a lot of shelves and piled them high with lengths of what she erroneously termed wools and silks. Inquisitive as usual, I went in and bought a whole lot of stuff I had absolutely no use for, as always paying the price for wanting to be liked. In less time than it took to draw breath, I volunteered, because she was homeless, and with the Greeks having just departed, that she could rent Buntings.

That was the biggest mistake of my landlady phase. She was a desperate, lonely drunk, tormented by agonizing self-pity, and absolutely lost even in semi-rural Sussex society. I genuinely wished I had been more compassionate, listened more. She was so huge, so unhappy, so dreadfully alone. I think she came from Hollywood, had in a way been on the fringe of what she constantly called Show Business, trying to strike a sort of 'We know, don't we?' spark of intimacy in me. She had fetched up in England because there was a daughter married to a North Countryman. This couple once came to see her, made it clear that was the last thing in life they wanted to do, and vanished, leaving her in a slough of booze and tears. If I had the power to write about real loneliness, the story would be entitled 'Dale'.

Alas, I was too harassed and selfishly taken up with my own problems to comfort her. She exasperated me, and the culminating straw was pages and pages of what she called film and television scripts, tapped out on her typewriter at night. Each one was more awful than the last, but she knew for certain, if only I could see it, that somewhere was another *Gone with the Wind*. I do wish I could have seen it, but I could not. What I did see was filth and dirt and unwashed dishes piling up everywhere and my little cottage becoming my little slum dwelling. I cannot remember how I did it (I never remember anything ruthless and tough I have done, I blot out such things), but I did it just the same; I told her she must go. I avoided telling her that it was possible that, as she was a sitting tenant, I had no right to do this. But she accepted the decision and made me feel very bad as she gave me masses of her material – she had nowhere to take it.

It all smelled dreadfully of stale cigarette smoke, so after I had pushed this old American, ex-show girl into a taxi to take her to Haywards Heath station, I burned it in my garden. After that, where? I do not know, I am ashamed I did not care, and as I danced round the bonfire I had made, I kept chanting, 'Am I my brother's keeper?' and decided, in this case, definitely not.

I am still appalled that I could be so hard. Everything at Buntings, where I live now, had to be burned, and that included beds and bedlinen, curtains and carpets. The Council had to be asked to make arrangements to fumigate the place, even cooking utensils made their way to the dustbin. The walls were stripped and the house repainted. After months of effort it looked new and very attractive. I was completely broke; Eaton Square had gone, Cornwall had gone. I shrugged my shoulders. What did such things really matter? It was at that moment I knew the right buyer would turn up and Ockenden Cottage would be sold and I would live at Buntings for six months. All this happened exactly as I visualized, except that six months has become eleven years and I am still here. My sons turn up when they have a mind to, having grumbled a bit about my leaving the house that they surprised me by telling me was the home they loved and cared about, but there is a difference – I am ten grandchildren better off. They turn up too, usually when they are least expected and there are not enough beds to go round.

It is only now that I know that selling the house at Fowey in Cornwall was the saddest decision of all. I still regret doing it – it was the dream holiday home for the now huge Fox family. Robin and his elder sister Mary designed a simple house themselves one wet afternoon, took the drawing to a local builder, and put the work in hand. They decided on four bedrooms, two bathrooms, a big kitchen dining-room and a big sitting-room with huge windows looking out to Readymoney Cove, and taking in some of the magical view of the harbour and Polruan, the village on the opposite shore.

We had a motorboat, looked after by Ernie, who worked for us. Robert's joy in the school holidays was to go fishing before breakfast – he used to come back with enough mackerel to feed a regiment. This was a calm and peaceful time for Robin and me and for his sister. The ground we bought was adjacent to her home; it was all very Foxy – but there were no outsiders invited, no London boat-rockers invited to play their hand. I know I was happier there than I had ever been with him, and I know he was happy too. He and Mary established a really good relationship and together they bought a stretch of river and so had good salmon fishing – the hobby and joy of both their lives. Cocky Farr, a keen fisherman, often joined us – they would return from the river long after dark, just occasionally, only very occasionally, with a salmon – but they had known huge enjoyment.

I went to the house several times after Robin died – but the fun had gone out of things. Now I wish I had not made the hasty decision to sell.

10

Up for Sale

That black day I had read by chance in the *Evening Standard*,
'The Estate of Robin Fox, Theatrical Impresario – NIL', I
was still playing Lady Bountiful from London, and gave my
dear old half-a-day-a-week gardener in Cornwall, who had
been the local dustman, called Wellington, the car I used
there. Oh the largesse, was there no end to my play-acting?
I left Eaton Square, giving the boys any furniture and pictures
they really wanted, and leaving behind curtains and carpets
for which their father had paid a fortune. Knowing how rich
the man is who lives there now, they will, no doubt, have
ended up on a skip. Now, Ockenden Cottage, Cuckfield –
that must go. I must start on that much talked-about game
called 'cutting your coat according to the cloth'. If I sold it,
I would have just enough money to bring me in a very small
income. A friend of many years' standing wanted it, we liked
each other, trusted each other, we shook hands on the deal
– 'SOLD' – the home of my family, the scene of love and
hate, of birth and death, the background to our lives, our
laughter and our tears, gone on the shake of this hand.

It is strange, I now live across the courtyard. I see Ockenden Cottage when I draw the curtains in the morning, I see it when I close them at night. I have never had one second of regret. Of course a home of so many years was packed with memories, and the 'never look back' theme could be heard strumming in the background, but mostly as an accompaniment to the sound of friends' voices, and the clatter of the boys and their friends growing up.

The business of moving three rather over-furnished homes into one small one would have been daunting, except that willing hands cropped up in every direction, and the exercise soon got under way. Edward, James and Robert were working, and I knew more or less which bits and pieces each one would like for their own homes. James had left some very nice things with me to look after for him when he gave up his London house, but he and Mary did not want them – of all the family I admired his taste the most and was puzzled by this rejection, but quickly realized they were setting out to build a new life together, and this they have done.

There is little doubt that it would have taken less energy on my part to move to Timbuctoo than it took to make the crossing over what the Foxes called the courtyard from Ockenden Cottage to Buntings.

Our home since 1939 had really ceased to be a cottage in 1969. Up till then we had been semi-detached. The other part of the building to which our cottage had been attached was the bakery and the shop which went with it. All the bread eaten in our village and most of the surrounding villages was baked on the premises. This had been so for as long as anyone could remember. Around 4 a.m. each morning muffled noises could be heard as the first mixing of the dough got under way. This was always done by hand. Shortly after that, the smell of yeast and baking loaves filled the morning air.

Our starry film friends, when they were staying with us, thought this 'Just Great', as they had probably only known sliced white rubbish packed in Cellophane. I used to have to warn them never to go downstairs at night as the burglar alarm would go off. In fact, we had no such alarm, but, from next door, when the human beings staying with us had retired to bed, vast armies of beetles would move in. The floor of our kitchen would become a moving black mass, as if they were having a huge party. I fought this sinister throng, which I was told was harmless, with all the strength at my disposal, but, as far as I could see, I failed 100 per cent to affect the life of even one beetle.

We grew tired of the beetles and of the smell, but when, after many years, the baker decided to throw in his hand because competition was threatening – the village grocer had been bought by a supermarket chain – we were sad. We would miss the bakery – especially the rolls straight out of the oven every morning for breakfast and the doughnuts for elevenses.

But over the years, too, Robin and the baker had passed the time of day together; they had an understanding that, if and when he thought of selling up, we would be the first to know. That day came. Dressed to the nines, even to the inclusion of a smart Homburg hat perched on top of his bald head which he did not remove when he made his call, the baker made a good picture as a businessman. We had never seen him before except in a collarless shirt, with sleeves rolled up, and a white – or what started out as white – apron tied round the waist with a coarse bit of string. But it was a very smart gentleman who appeared at the front door that Sunday morning.

Fortunately Robin was in, and they disappeared to the one sitting-room that we had at that time. About ten minutes passed and, on the shake of a hand, the bakery was ours.

Here the smooth, rural life part of the story stops, because, by now, we had some money. Robin had made a success. He was one of the most famous international theatrical agents in the world. I had become the typical wife who loved acquiring and altering houses, and so a medieval cottage in a village street with a pretty garden became a real house, and very lovely it was too in a way, and I was constantly praised for the beautiful home I had created. It is always nice to be praised, but I knew that we had spent a fortune on what had not really been necessary. Some rather charming old features I had actually destroyed. I was to blame: Robin had left everything to me.

The part of the building where the bread was baked, including the ovens, had been there such a long time that it was of historic interest. How could I have been so hasty? I disposed of all that and put in a double garage. The shop where the bread was sold came off better. The Victorians had disguised its age with thick plaster, which we had torn off to expose and reveal the beautiful wooden beams beneath. Robin did not really like the architecture of that period, he would have preferred an eighteenth-century manor house. I joined him in loathing dark beams, which were in danger of becoming an over-riding feature of the whole building. So we had them all stripped back to their original timber shade of honey. Some had been there since about 1100. Taking off the dark-brown stain and leaving them as they were originally was a real success, but it meant spending money at the millionaire level.

But suddenly the cottage became a substantial house, with seven bedrooms and three bathrooms, two kitchens and three sitting-rooms. Robin used one of the sitting-rooms as a small library and work room, for he was constantly having to telephone all over the world – particularly at weekends, it seemed. If the telephone did stop for a minute, he could relax up there, away from the rest of the family, who were always swarming over the house with their friends.

To reach what received the gracious title of the main drawing-room meant coming down a large and very pretty staircase, which we had installed, into the central hall, now a big room which joined the two premises together. I had found mellow bricks being torn from the pavements of a village near Herstmonceaux. I bought them and used them for the floor of this hall, and we installed heating underneath, so we were never cold. The effect of the soft colour of the floor, with the honey-coloured beams, was near perfect.

The drawing-room was really large and we made a drinks cupboard off it to one side so disguised that only we knew it was there . . . nothing so vulgar as drinks on view. The downstairs cloakroom leading off the hall was bigger than the sitting-room I am writing in at this moment.

Robin and I both started off in high spirits. We designed this new house together, without the help of an architect. That was no problem as we did have an excellent builder whom we knew through Elaine Blond of the Marks & Spencer family. This builder did everything for her on her estate at East Grinstead. I was having such a good time and enjoying everything so much. Every room was covered with samples of expensive materials for curtains, chair covers, and so on. At first Robin appeared to enjoy all of this as much as I did. Then I observed that he looked tired and appeared suddenly to be apathetic. I realized that he was over-working and my interior decorator fantasy was possibly growing monotonous. I decided to let up a bit, and to make more decisions on my own, to let him have some peace.

He came home one night to this house in a state of shambles. He looked utterly exhausted. 'What sort of day have you had?'

'Not good. I have had an X-ray. I have a shadow on my lung.' In nine months exactly to the day he was dead.

I think he and I were both moderately creative people. We loved beautiful things and wanted to express this love. At the end of his life, when he had succeeded, he now loathed his success, detested being a theatrical agent, although so many great stars wanted his help and his friendship, and he would say nearly every day, 'Oh I wish I could get out of this life!'

When Robin looked at Buntings, where I live now, all he ever saw were two derelict cottages. They belonged to the baker, whose son lived in one and, when the son left to marry, Robin bought it for less than three thousand pounds, telling me that we would buy the other one too as soon as it became empty. I am sure he saw as clearly as I did what it could be like, so, perhaps if he walked in today, he would not be surprised.

11

Feet on the Ground

When the baker and his wife, who had helped him by serving in the shop from 9 a.m. to 5 p.m. every day, with no other help at all, moved lock, stock and barrel to a neat, ultra-modern house on the edge of Cuckfield, the village where they had served us faithfully for so many years, they took with them their secrets of home-baked bread and buns and cakes. We miss them every day. I used to wonder if we were popular hosts to so many because of the absence in our house of the dead packets of sliced bread.

The loaves, still warm, were served to guests sitting at a scrubbed kitchen table in an alcove with a big window shaped like half a wheel, looking out on the garden that my sister, Elizabeth, had helped me transform so many years ago when it was the village rubbish dump. Many dreams for films and plays that later became realities were thought up round that table, with non-stop fresh coffee made by Mary – who is still spoiling me at Buntings – and home-made marmalade, which I am proud to say was made by me.

When Mr King, the baker, and Mrs King swapped the

character, even the beauty, of the ancient bakery for a neat little suburban residence, they removed an important part of traditional village life and took a dying skill with them. They had meant so much for so many years to one woman that I think she actually died because of their decision. This was Flo. She lived in the cottage that was semi-detached from the one Robin had bought. Our half was now empty and getting more decayed and derelict every day, but Flo and her greyhound had lived in the other half for as many years as we had been at Ockenden Cottage.

With Flo still living there I succeeded in buying her house for a few thousand pounds. I never charged her any rent because I knew, as she worked for the baker, that she had never paid rent before. Nothing would have induced me to try to make her leave. This was her home of a lifetime. I never really thought at that time that Buntings would become a reality because Flo was strong, tough and aggressive, and she drove the baker's van and delivered the loaves and cakes throughout the district with her greyhound, her companion, always sitting beside her.

She was a well-known and respected figure in the village because she was the Ian Botham of Cuckfield stoolball team. Naturally we collected our own bread and I never knew Flo well. Also, she was often rude and she frightened the day-lights out of me. She was large, masculine, with crew-cut hair. She worked from dawn till dusk loading the trays and delivering. I thought that she was contented with her lot and indestructible.

How wrong, how patronizing, how unobservant of me. The baker left and with him went his van which, for a lifetime, she had driven. This van must have been really more her and her dog's home than the cottage in which they lived, because, from the day the baker moved and she stopped driving the van, her personality, her appearance – even her aggressive manner – faded in front of our eyes. Physically she shrank to a shadow of herself. I am certain that with the departure of her world her heart was broken. The dog, too, became pitifully thin. I saw her often enough to feel deep concern, but the dog was a constant reminder of how little we do for each other, unless for some reason it suits us. He sat at a window every day – one that now looks out on my charming courtyard – barking feebly, but more often howling, and then whimpering in misery.

Finally I could no longer bear seeing the plight they were in. I tackled one of the doctors, a partner in the sort of medical combine the general public have to suffer today. He shrugged his shoulders and said she was not too well. I knew she had diabetes, didn't I? I did not, how could I? There was nothing he could do. If he talked to her she would not listen. Probably true, but I hated the fact that he was a member of a profession that I recall from experience was once full of men selflessly dedicated to helping and healing and who never thought of financial reimbursement.

Now this young man, quite typical of doctors today, drawing a very good salary long before he had any practical experience, was shaking off any responsibility for Flo, his patient, who, of course, like all of us, had paid the insurance which made up his salary.

I next went to seek the RSPCA in Horsham about the dog. It proved to me that I would rather be an ill animal than an ill human being. I was listened to politely and by the time I returned home a kind man had gone ahead and was

8 Cecil Beaton, James and Lady Diana Duff Cooper at the party after the première of *Thoroughly Modern Millie*, 1967

9 Robert

10 Robert Morley at my seventieth birthday party, 1982

11 Mrs Neville Blond
12 Anthony Pelissier and his wife Ursula Howells, 1987

13 Buntings before . . . in its bakery days
14 And after . . . my home now for eleven years
15 My garden at Buntings

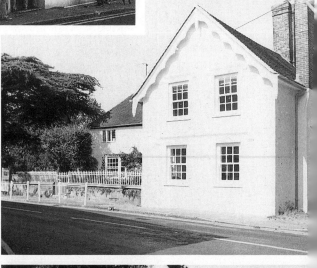

already examining the dog. He must have been clever and tactful, too, as Flo had actually let him in! Perhaps she was relieved to have help at last.

After a while he came across the courtyard to me, and confirmed my worst fears. The poor, sad dog was in a parlous state. Very old age was probably playing a big part, but the animal was nearly starving and it was too late to do anything.

'He must be put down,' said the RSPCA officer.

'No way,' I shouted. 'He is all Flo has on earth.'

The RSPCA gentleman was firm, polite. 'You must see Miss Flo and reason with her.'

'Don't joke, she would see me on my way with language I can't use in front of you.'

'You came to the RSPCA. You have heard what can be our only opinion. No doubt you will talk to the lady and she will see what has to be done. She isn't a cruel person.' He gave me a card with his name on it, jumped in his car, assuring me as he moved off that the beloved greyhound would be collected and would not suffer. Oh no? How could he be sure?

'Let me know,' he called as he was vanishing. 'Let me know what you decide.' I know what I had decided, as I have so often when there is nothing else to do.

'I'll pray to God,' I shouted back at him. I should like to have added, 'You're putting Flo down, too, you know.'

My prayer was answered that very evening. It was Flo who was admitted to hospital, Flo who died of her broken heart.

When my RSPCA friend came back, he said, 'I knew you would do the right thing.'

'Well,' I said, 'it wasn't exactly me. I can't take all the credit, but that is a long story and not for now.'

He lifted the dog with such tenderness into the car that the animal seemed resigned and lay quietly in a comfortable basket that he would lie in for his last car ride.

They shot down the alleyway, the route that he and Flo had taken for so many years on their rounds. I cried unashamedly, turned back to look at the two cottages, the derelict ruins that were now mine. 'What shall I do with them?' Again I dare to think this question was answered. Anyway, here I am living rather comfortably, and Buntings, which emerged from these ruins, is a home for me and anyone who cares to turn up, a stopping-off place for my family when it suits them, and for the many friends that arrive from different parts of the globe.

*

When the sale of Ockenden Cottage was agreed, part of the deal was that the kitchen garden went with my bit. It had always been called 'the cabbage patch', and still is, and what really matters is that indoors and outside the whole thing is, in fact, the creation of many friends who planned and worked most selflessly to turn this ruin into a home. I did not do it on my own. I was never alone, never without help, and that is still the case.

In the other house I had had a cook for years, my dear Alice. The first thing that happened was that her husband, always known as 'My Sid' because this was how she referred to him, built a wall. Sid, a master bricklayer who had worked for many years for the best local builder's, found old bricks with lovely colours, so the wall looked as if it had been there since the beginning of time. He curved it round the cabbage

patch, so just to look out on it is a great pleasure. Best of all
is the fact that it divides the properties – and better still the
new owner of Ockenden Cottage paid for it!

It was in 1977 that an enjoyable task began. It was the
turning of the two derelict cottages into the home that it is
now. I met, through my sister, Anne Morice – still referred
to by us all as Nutkin, the label Nanny gave her in the
nursery all those years ago – an architect who had enlarged
her house at Hambeldon, near Henley. Her name was
Barbara Cook. Strangely, she was a Russian, and she lived
nearby. When I was staying with my sister, she invited her
to lunch, and, on sight, I liked her so much that I begged
her to bring her skills to restoring the dark hovel haunting
me in Cuckfield. I never regretted this, though she may have
done, continually making long journeys cross-country from
Henley to Sussex. Only when the job was completed did I
learn that she was a very sick woman. Alas, this clever lady
died soon after the job of showing me what could be done
by expertise and hard work. What she accomplished gives
me pleasure every day. My old-fashioned, rather contemptu-
ous and ill-informed attitude to 'the professional woman',
my 'all men can do anything well' speech, vanished for
ever.

A local building firm, of men, of course, was engaged,
and, one day, when the ruin was nearly a house, they told
me that in no way was it possible to put in a hot-water system
with the main supply tank upstairs. 'You'll have to put a
bathroom downstairs.'

'Where? In the kitchen? In the sitting-room? That is not
on. It doesn't suit my picture of gracious living, and anyway
there isn't room to swing a cat.'

'You'll have to try, there is no alternative,' said the builders.

'We shall see, I will telephone Mrs Cook.' Barbara answered my SOS. She arrived post-haste, and in no time she had a team of sulking, resentful men cutting a large hole in the kitchen ceiling in order to hoist, with immense difficulty, a heavy tank up to the bathroom where she knew there was space to house it. With much puffing and blowing and cursing, this was achieved and experienced men were proved wrong – as well as bone idle, which we both knew they were.

Another brilliant stroke on her part was to notice a skip in her village street. On it she spied a Georgian bow window – a period house opposite her own was being destroyed to make way for a batch of modern monstrosities termed a Housing Estate. This disgusting trade is in the hands of men called property developers. I think they are a virus, a disease, against which there is no antibiotic as yet. Barbara bought this window for five pounds, and turned an ugly square box which, up to then, was called a living-room, into a pretty sitting-room looking out to a small, picturebook flower garden which had been the kitchen garden of Ockenden Cottage.

Barbara was, of course, a professional. Someone who was famous for being very charming, although said to be tremendously selfish and egocentric, but who did just as much for me with absolutely no thought of himself, was Anthony Pelissier. By the time he came back into my life he was a very good film director, with a number of excellent pictures to his credit, notably *The Rocking Horse Winner* and *Mr Polly*, starring his friend, John Mills. We had re-established our friendship because Tracey Reed, my son Edward's first wife, was his daughter. Anthony had married her mother, Penelope Dudley-Ward, during the war and, like many such marriages, it ended with that war. 'Pempey', as she was always called, married Carol Reed, the film director. Anthony faded from the picture, rather typical of him. Carol assumed the paternal role, and very well he did it.

I like to think that it was through the Foxes that Tracey and her real father re-established the affectionate relationship they now have, making quite an ordinary, to-be-expected picture. At Edward and Tracey's wedding, Carol had been the father figure. Anthony had disappeared from all our lives, and, later, when their marriage foundered, it was always to Carol that I turned when I went through periods of great distress concerning Lucy, my granddaughter. I wish he was alive to turn to now. He was a brilliant man with a charismatic personality. I loved him and Pempey very much.

But when Anthony reappeared on the scene, I loved him too. We re-established immediately the platonic friendship we had enjoyed as penniless teenagers. Of course I cannot be flattering him when, as I tell him constantly, I so enjoy his company, so understand what he means, and feel as if I have a brother. I feel that he *is* my brother. He is the most intelligent friend I have ever had. His advice to others is always balanced, thoughtful and sound, but he is the perfect example of a person being 'his own worst enemy'. This is possibly because he is honest, will not flatter, will not compromise in his likes, particularly in his dislikes, and he accumulates an awful lot of these. So, as a result, he has not fully realized any of his gifts. He is very musical, very well read, a particularly fine and sensitive photographer, and some of my favourite paintings are his work. He is painstaking and methodical.

I have often heard the term lazy connected with him. This must come from people who foolishly expect from him more than they were ever going to get. There is no doubt he can be very, very difficult. That amuses me. Why shouldn't it? He has never been difficult with me. I enjoy every moment of his company, I find him full of worldly wisdom. Not only do I ask his advice, more often than not I take it. And more to him than to anyone else do I owe my garden at Buntings.

From an ugly patch of ground, with an outside privy at the end of it, he created a trellised courtyard which is a real joy. I had picked up four beautiful lead doves in a junkyard some years previously, and he used these on four quite unpretentious columns. He made enough room for two flowerbeds, which we packed with bulbs for the spring. There is a flowering cherry tree and, climbing up the trellis, we have roses and clematis, jasmine and vines. Sometimes I am overwhelmed because everything grows so prolifically, and I am taken to task by the gardener who has to check and tidy back the results of Anthony's suggestions.

So many people enjoy all this rather overgrown muddle, and it was entirely created by Anthony. He makes good shapes for me and then uses the theatrical term, 'Oh get on, you dress the set.' I never even buy a chair for the garden unless I think, 'Would Anthony like it?' and if I can answer 'Yes', then the chair comes home with me. Anthony's work is all done on paper, and he will explain what he means to others, who do the practical work. I doubt if he has ever done such a thing in a garden as even plant one snowdrop himself. He never pretended that manual labour would have done anything other than bore him.

Anthony made exactly the right shapes. One weekend Edward, in a rage and entirely against his will – it not being his scene at all – laid the lawn for me because some turf had been delivered that was going to be useless unless it was put down the very moment it arrived. Edward had been about to leave for London. The fact that with bad grace he did as his mother beseeched him very nearly destroyed our mother and son relationship.

There are plants everywhere, with an accent on old-fashioned roses. I spend a great deal more time, but less money, in nursery gardens than anyone I know, because whenever I get the question from my many friends and huge family, 'What do you want for your birthday? What do you want for Christmas?', it is always the same answer, 'Something for the garden.' Everything I am given is planted, nothing is thrown away, and I certainly would never get a prize for design at Chelsea. For those who do not like a blaze of colour in the summer, I beg them not to visit.

Buntings was to have been a temporary bolt hole. But now I am the forever enchanted owner of this patch, as I have been of other patches. It has two double bedrooms and a single one, and, as I have said, a wonderful hot-water system, and the loft, which once was too dark and dirty to enter except on all-fours because the roof had fallen in, is now a lovely room running the length of the cottage. As Barbara built out enormous windows it makes a splendid work-room and I can boast that everyone falls in love with it. The windows that face south look over medieval rooftops right to Chanctonbury Ring, and a west-facing window looks out not only to my garden, but to many other surrounding gardens, and through the trees to Ockenden Manor, a magnificent Elizabethan house, now naturally a hotel.

The sitting-room window frames the garden, and, in summer, with all the windows open, becomes a part of it. In winter, as I am writing now, there is an open fire. On shelves created by Barbara are housed all my favourite books, with room amongst them, almost hidden, for a Japanese stereo radio and gramophone, so there can be music whenever the mood steals over me. This sort of instrument is mysterious magic to me, but I have a young friend who maintains it for me, takes trouble with the speakers, and keeps it working perfectly, and the acoustics in this small room are good. One way that my sons spoil me is by giving me many of the latest records and cassettes . . . and, of course, there is the ghastly goggle box, which I can hide, even pretend I do not care for much, but, of course, the moment I am alone, I am glued to the dreary, depressing news, and the dreaded *Wogan*, and suchlike, with fifty million other addicts.

PART FOUR

12

She Lived in a Shoe

I find it intriguing the way men and women talk about their offspring, even when those in question are middle-aged people. Nearly always they refer to them as 'the children' and with an authority and a certainty about their characters and problems – as if anything could be known with such certainty. Unless I am an exception to the rule, most parents are living in a dream world. I play the game too, and have to remind myself that I am being observed. Love between parents and their children is something that I learned cannot be taken for granted. I was once very disturbed about a child who I thought was being misunderstood by his mother and father. I went with my problem to a paediatrician friend to whom I was forever turning for advice. 'Phillip,' I said, 'this child is unhappy. They are positively cruel in their lack of understanding.'

Phillip looked at me over the top of his glasses with a quizzical, slightly pitying expression. 'Do they love the child?'

'Phillip, I am talking about the boy's mother and father.'

'I know that, but love, even from parents, is more rare than you seem to realize.'

I think I can say that I loved Edward, William, later to be James, and Robert as much as I am capable of feeling this emotion, and we are a united team to this day. Of course I annoy and irritate them often, and, alas, probably disappoint them. All three, at times, have surprised, amazed and disturbed me and taught me to know despair. But that, I am sure, was due to my own lack of awareness and understanding of their natures and needs. Like most parents, I painted the picture I wanted to see and was determined on them being as I saw them in a dream. I now accept all this as pretty run of the mill and I struggle, not always successfully, not to dramatize the fact. I wonder if being childless is so sad if it means escaping the pain and the tears that are shed by all parents when, sooner or later, the children bring home to them that they have failed, and that life is not made up of days of seeing our progeny winning first prize.

Edward has surprised me at every level. He was not a problem child – no moods, no tantrums, or so it seemed. But in his early twenties he suffered such intense unhappiness I loathed myself for ever having had a child, and so being the cause of a human being living in such misery. But, of course, I know now he could never have become the fine actor that he is, and portray such poetry and pain that he can share with an audience, unless he had lived through pain himself.

William knocked me for six. He was my handsome, naughty extrovert, unbeatable, unflappable, full of wicked laughter, and so on. Everything was a joke, nothing was taken seriously and the expression 'he could charm the birds

off the trees' really did apply to him. I never had to worry
about him, he went his own way, was very self-sufficient,
very good at games, never did any work and had a whale of
a good time at home and at Harrow and later when he joined
the Coldstream Guards to do his National Service.

Success came, I think, and so, I believe, did he, with the
film *The Servant*. To get such generous support as he did
from Dirk Bogarde does not happen to many young actors.
His life changed quite literally overnight. Suddenly he was
a star and offers of work involving money that he can never
have dreamed of came rolling in. He had been deeply in
love with Sarah Miles, who was in *The Servant* with him,
ever since they were students. She had been at RADA, he
at the Central School of Speech and Drama where he was
a contemporary of Vanessa Redgrave. But when he was
suddenly famous their love affair, so important to him, hit
the rocks, and Sarah, of whom I was – and still am – fond,
saw that he paid a cruel price for outstripping her in the
game at which she was so determined to succeed. But he
did not outstrip her intentionally. He loved her.

He was emotionally distressed for the first time in his life
when he went to Hollywood to play in *Thoroughly Modern
Millie* with Julie Andrews. But it was when his father and I
were there and he was making *King Rat*, directed by Bryan
Forbes, that our world, that is the world concerning our
children, collapsed and dissolved in misery. This was when
we recognized as we saw him enter a typical Hollywood
party, that he had fallen a victim to the drug scene that was
beginning to take over the young and beautiful working in
films at that time. His father was deeply unhappy and so, of
course, was I, but I was more optimistic by nature, perhaps.

I thought he would discard drugs before they became a habit: I had thought of him as a strong character.

My faith in him proved right. He was helped, I am sure, by his wife, Mary. It was difficult for us to know what to make of their Born Again Christianity, but we could see that she represented all that he needed most. We were – and I still am – convinced that he was brought up in the Christian faith, and I remember Robin and I becoming quite serious for a moment when he was confirmed at Harrow. We felt, perhaps, we had not done a very good job because he did not seem to be taking the occasion seriously. I know that on the drive home we talked at length about this, knowing how important faith should be in all our lives. We agreed that confirmation generally took place when people were very immature and we wondered whether this important event should not, in fact, be at the end of their schooling when they were beginning to think seriously for themselves. Religion would then not be imposed upon them as a convention and at a time convenient to a bishop whose programme was probably too full.

*

Edward, James and Robert have ten childen between them, so when they all turn up at once I am indeed 'the old woman who lived in a shoe', Buntings being that size. I observe with pleasure three good fathers. Difficulties, of course, have occurred in their domestic lives. They are human. But with all three of them the children come first. Robin suffered a sense of insecurity when his overwhelming parents were suddenly involved in divorce, and, try as my mother would to do her very best for me, with Freddie Lonsdale as a father, being wanted by either of them was not on the agenda. Very occasionally Robin and I would admit to each other how terribly insecure we felt, so perhaps our boys have benefited by these early traumas which we went through.

I am often asked, 'And what are the boys doing now?' The answer is easy, but seldom understood. 'As I am their mother, I naturally have not the faintest idea.' How disappointing of me. They are, by nature, perhaps by upbringing, men who play their cards close to the chest, and they tell me exactly what they think is good for me and that is all, and I do not believe that, until this moment, I have ever admitted that that goes for me too. I seem, I know, to talk non-stop, but never, under any circumstances, do I tell my right hand what my left hand is doing. Of course, they tell me what work they intend to have a try at when the deals concerning it are sealed and signed, and when the team that they will be working with is in the picture. But they are busy men, and quite often I will read of their plans in a newspaper before they have ever been mentioned to me.

Robert communicates most easily of the three and will occasionally include me by sometimes, when he is staying with me, tossing me over a script to read. We can agree about a play – often we disagree – and we will enjoy casting it in our minds, only to see that we were barking up the wrong tree when it falls into the hands of the director.

My sons' private lives we never mention, though gossip can drift my way. If, of course, they are about to be married, then they have to put me in the picture, so that I can assemble my mother-in-law role, a part I have played quite often, and with great pleasure. I love all my daughters-in-law. They are very interesting girls and most tolerant of me, and there have been quite a number of them. James is the least married – just once so far. But then he did bring a fleet of beautiful girls home before he settled for his wife, Mary.

Edward married Tracey Reed, Freda Dudley-Ward's granddaughter, when they were very, very young. This ended in tears all round, but they had a lovely daughter, Lucy, and, for the past three years, I have had reason to see that those tears were futile and unnecessary. Lucy, looking most beautiful, was married two years ago to David Grenfell. She was given away by her father – who, incidentally, insists that Tracey must always be present at his first nights – and this erstwhile daughter-in-law Tracey held my hand very tight all through the ceremony. There were, of course, tears in our eyes then, for different reasons. We have matured and we played our conventional roles, grandmother and mother of the bride, to the hilt.

Joanna David was the next girl for Edward, that is, the next official one, the mother of my granddaughter Emilia, who shows signs of being a musician, music being her father's first love. She won a scholarship in the subject at the Frances Holland School, and has now gone to Bryanston. Joanna causes me to boast that I have the perfect daughter-in-law, kind, considerate, generous, domesticated, a great companion, and, best of all, she can be wickedly and unexpectedly funny.

James's wife, Mary, has had the worst of me. A nicer girl one could not meet. Her strength is that she was not brought up in our theatrical world, and a great deal of the time, since James abandoned evangelism and returned to that scene, I think she has not the faintest idea what we are talking about.

This does not stop her loving him dearly and being a good mother to five ebullient children. She has many virtues absent from my make-up, including the power of forgiveness. This is especially admirable, as my behaviour towards their evangelical beliefs has been intolerant, to put it mildly.

James and Mary give their personal lives devotedly to their five children, so there are no nannies, no going away to prep school for this bright lot. They dominate the house with a noise that only five lively children can make. Perhaps a psychologist would tell me that James's recollection of his childhood was of unhappiness. I myself have known him actually accuse me of snobbish cruelty in that I sent him away to prep school and, later, to Harrow, simply to satisfy some desire in me for self-aggrandisement, causing him, he assures me, to be very unhappy. Harrow, he insists, when he is in an 'Anti Mother's Values' mood, really took the prize for cruelty: a school where there was a complete lack of understanding.

Our visions of the past differ here. He always appeared to be enjoying life to the full at Harrow on the Hill. He was a very good games player and seemed a most popular boy. I visited him often, caught my death of cold watching him play games, and took him and his friends out to enormous meals of sausages and doughnuts and Mars bars. The fun always seemed fast and furious. Robin's and my worry was about the difficulty in raising the money to pay huge fees to provide him with the best education that, as we saw it, money could buy. Actually, we would feel a bit irritated, even harassed, by the fact that he never did a stroke of work, but we shrugged our shoulders. He was a fine-looking boy, and

Robin always said that if schoolmasters could not engage the average child's interest, it was their fault, and there were other values to be gained from his old school. I agreed, and together we set about mustering the fees. I bought antiques for Jules Stein, of MCA, for his offices all over the world, and later I had a shop in Beauchamp Place with Lord Middleton. Robert now has very nice offices opposite where this struggle took place, and life has gone round in yet another circle.

But recently James informed me that he has put his sons down for Harrow, which he thinks is a damned good school. He asks me very seriously, 'What are you laughing at, Ma?'

I am rather a detached grandmother. I have already admitted that my maternal instincts are a bit patchy. That is, if the children are well and rampageous and doing their own scene. If they are not well, of course I feel concerned, and there are no ends I would not go to to help materially, if it became necessary.

James and Mary's eldest son, Tom, was the victim of a very rare and serious illness in 1986. All that I could do then was to feel concern for all three of them, and so see the fortitude and discipline and, of course, love that was brought to this problem, which did have a happy ending. Thomas was cared for and cured under the NHS. Nowhere in the world could he have had better care. I admired Mary's calmness and the personal relationship founded on respect that was established between her and the surgeon who operated on Thomas, and the nurses responsible for his aftercare.

I remembered the time that my youngest son, Robert, was rushed to Great Ormond Street Hospital with a fractured skull. I am sure I did not behave as well as Mary, and her good behaviour caused me to regret, yet again, how badly I had behaved on the occasion of her marriage to James.

I visited James and his wife in Sheffield just after Thomas was born. I did not recognize the father of the baby as anyone I knew. He bore no relation to the son I thought I had. I had been to see and pay authorities in the world of drug-prevention to explain why this was. Had I imagined it? Was there anything I could do?

'No,' said these wise fellows. 'What he took causes changes of personality irrevocably, incurably.'

Out came my cheque book. In a short space of time, however, I knew I had wasted my money. They were one hundred per cent wrong. After a few years James decided that he should act again and the agent who had shown him loyalty for twelve years was the first on his casualty list. He had a chance to play in *A Passage to India*, and who better to advise him and make a really good deal than his brother, Robert? The film was a success and he was a Name once more.

But I was not to be let off being irritated, to put it mildly, by a performance he may have kept just for me. He became the humble fellow, not versed in the ways of the world, when he telephoned me one day and said, 'Ma, I would like to give a thank-you party for David Lean. I owe him so much for the trouble he took directing me in the picture. What do you advise me to do?'

'Ring up the Savoy Grill and book a table.'

'Oh, will you do it for me? They will not know who I am.'

'Now don't play that game with me. You've spent a fortune there in the past, enough to keep the lot of us, and you know very well that you were in the Coldstream with Giles Shepherd who now runs the hotel.'

No more humble-pie nonsense came my way for a while and I was invited to the dinner, as were his brothers and their wives, for the Foxes to honour a great director.

We had the best table, as I knew we would. We had more waiters to serve us than there were guests. The dinner and the wine were ordered by James before we arrived, because he knew David Lean's taste. It was all perfect and we had an enjoyable evening. He put me next to David Lean. No one is easy, and I was glad I was not an actress, so that I could just enjoy the company of this very intelligent man of my own generation. James was the perfect host. He may irritate me often – he probably means to, that is what mothers are for – but I shall not be fooled again by the portrayal of the simple fellow out of touch with the wicked ways of the world, in which others, including me, he considers such dab hands. He has renounced the devil – we have not. Nonsense, it is not as easy as that. The devil has many tricks up his sleeve.

Thinking of my sons, I see them like a bunch of beautiful balloons that I am holding in my hand at a party, and one by one they burst in my face. I still love balloons, but I have far less confidence in party going.

Edward's first marriage failed, simply, I think, because they were both too young, and I am sure that Robert's failed for the same reason. But from Edward and Tracey I am lucky enough to have a granddaughter, Lucy, and thanks to Robert and Celestia I have three more lovely grandchildren. They seem to be quite unaffected by anything that has happened. I sometimes think that I am the only one who feels a bit blue, but it is not my business, so I simply try to sit on the side-lines. My philosophy never varies – I simply leave the door open for whoever feels like walking through. Simon Marks used to say, 'Never destroy bridges, people may want to use them.'

13

Back on the Avenue

It was during a moment of escape from the Royal Court
Theatre Upstairs, when I was feeling no sympathy with,
or understanding of, the work being done there that I ran
into a young man called John Simpson who was managing
the theatre. I had been aware of him for some time, and
thought how well he did the job. I was trying to do
my 'escape unnoticed' scene after twenty minutes when he
politely asked me if I would like a drink. He did not know
anything about me or any of the connections that, through
my husband, I had had with the Royal Court. In the
(small) world of the theatre death makes the past immediately past. I saw my husband and his efforts and
his dreams everywhere. John Simpson had never heard of
Robin Fox.

Over a drink we looked forward, which is what I was
hoping to do. He told me of his hopes and aspirations. His
main interest was an idea he had to start an electrical
business. Strange that he should talk to me on this subject,
because all I am able to do is turn on an electric light –

provided I can find the switch. So we did not have all that much in common.

He needed some money to make his dream come true. For some reason, intuitively, I suppose, I believed in his ability, and, with immense difficulty, pinned down my Sole Executor to find a moment to write a cheque on my behalf to give to John Simpson. This I did, apologizing for it being such a small amount, and, when John thanked me, I said, 'Forget it. I shall. Good luck.'

John has dedicated himself to work and this has paid off. He is a big success. When he formed his electrical company, we agreed also that we would like to become a theatrical agency, one that would on no account represent actors – Robin had been an ace in that field, and I must never think that I could slip into his shoes. But John and I wanted to find and encourage directors and designers. That was in 1972. Since then I have become known as the dozing partner. This second venture simmered, while the electrical one grew and sparked. Then, three years ago, Wendy Toye asked me if I knew of any job in the administrative side of the theatre that would suit an English friend of hers. His name was David Watson. He had been a chorister, in fact he was the boy who sang the solo at the Coronation of Queen Elizabeth. Work had taken him to the United States and then family ties had made it necessary for him to return here.

David came to see me. I liked him so much that the catalyst in me was awakened and I gave him introductions to everyone I knew. It was a question of with whom did he feel he could work and – of course, as we are all human – who would pay the best money? One day I was sitting with him, mulling over a list we now had in our hands of exciting projects that had been suggested, when my intuitive feeling hit me again.

'Stop,' I shouted, 'we are being idiotic. I know that you must join my agency, Simpson Fox Associates.' I remember that moment vividly, because there was no hesitation. We shook hands there and then. We were both quite sure that that was what we wanted and we took this confidence to our first meeting with John.

There was an immediate understanding there, too, and in a very short time David was installed in a large cupboard off John's office in the Fulham Road – the only place available. His staff was a girl called Sheila Cassidy, who had been with John and me since the beginning.

David showed himself at once to be a shrewd workaholic. He was a born theatrical agent, and, best of all, he took to it as a duck to water, and was tremendously happy. He has built our agency in a short space of time into a big international success.

*

Early one evening in November 1987, I was standing at a window in an office in Shaftesbury Avenue. This was the new home of Simpson Fox Associates. David was still running it, joined recently by Anita Land, daughter of Leslie Grade, and sister of Michael. They were with me having a glass of champagne and the toast was 'Maggie', star of *Lettice and Lovage* produced by my son Robert. I asked them to turn out the lights and, as the room went dark, the brilliant advertisements flashing from the Globe Theatre opposite reflected into our room and shimmered on the walls and on the carpet.

As I looked down on the crowds waiting outside the theatre, I was so excited that my hand shook and I drank my champagne too quickly so that I did not spill it. Huge dark cars like black beetles crawled slowly to the front of the theatre and disgorged butterflies. These were the lucky ones who had first-night seats at the Globe Theatre to see brilliant Maggie Smith star in a play written especially for her by Peter Shaffer.

Standing where I was felt like a great moment in a long life. Do I believe in ghosts? I could say yes or no. I only knew, as I stood at that window and as I looked down, that Freddie Lonsdale was in the foyer and Glitters was in the crowd, watching the favoured going inside. Stranger still was the sensation that, although I was standing high up in that bow window, I was also down there with Glitters in the crowd and she and I were enjoying every moment as indeed we had done so often when I was young.

What a remarkable woman she was in many ways. No rancour, no bitterness at being on the outside looking in. We both enjoyed it all, even when it was a Frederick Lonsdale comedy that had made us take the bus from Victoria to join exactly the same crowd of people, it seemed, that I was watching that night. I was about eighteen years old again and just before one of his first nights Freddie had been attending a rehearsal and he had given me a few minutes in the foyer of this theatre.

I had been shaking that time while waiting but for a different reason, and with legitimate apprehension. I was going to see my father after many years and with any luck he was going to help me. I was an optimist.

He appeared with the great Ronald Squire, his leading

man, and he must have assessed my looks and general value as not too high. He just saw fit to give me an introduction to a not very distinguished manager of touring companies.

It was, of course, because of his name that I did get a job, the job that started my career in the theatre, and finally had me standing at the window on this November night, when Robert, the grandson of Glitters and Freddie Lonsdale, was presenting the play – a play that was unusual because for once we knew its success was assured even before the curtain went up.

I was brought back with a jolt from the past, back into the room. 'Come on,' said David and Anita. 'We must go to our seats. The curtain rises in five minutes.'

Down in the lift and across the road we went, pushing through the crowds outside and inside the theatre to our seats in the third row of the stalls. A bit of excited waving from first-night friends as we took our seats, very popular for at least one night in that mercurial society: the Foxes for however brief a moment spelt success.

Edward and James and their wives were sitting near me, and Edward had brought his daughter, Emilia. We were in our seats on time and up went the curtain, and there, on stage, was my dear friend, Maggie Smith, about to enchant an audience for three hours.

I was back on the Avenue, and certainly my sons were there with me and I am equally convinced that Freddie and Glitters were too.

*

Efficient David Grant, the Company Manager and an important man in Robert's team, collected us at the final curtain as the cheering was dying down, and took us through the pass door to Maggie's dressing-room. The exhausted star still found the energy to give the Foxes huge hugs of welcome, particularly my fourteen-year-old granddaughter, Emilia. I knew exactly how this made her feel, and that she will not forget that moment.

I suppose when I was young I used to fantasize about the stars. I did not know then that, when I grew up, I would get to know some very famous people well enough to see them and, indeed, love them dearly as real people. I regard myself as so lucky that my childish fantasies have come true, and the reality has been so wonderfully rewarding.

14

The True Performer

Laurence Olivier was a very young man when I was crying in Franz Lederer's dressing-room. I did not know him very well, but I remember being convinced he would never be an actor, least of all a star ... 'Too short,' I said, 'not very good-looking, nothing outstanding that I can see.'

I have never been a very intimate friend of Larry, in fact I knew Vivien Leigh much better when we were very young and before she met him, but there was a moment when he meant more to me than anyone. This was when my Sussex house, Ockenden Cottage, was deserted and silent after the avalanche of theatrical friends had gone on their way after the party that became, in a sense, the climax to my husband, Robin's, death – and to his funeral and life.

After the last guests had gone out on that January evening into a gale and blinding rain, I turned back to face what I dreaded: our big, empty sitting-room – emptiness and quiet were what I feared most, not only for myself, but for my sons, Edward, James and Robert, who were with me. I need never have felt this fear. Larry knew all the anguish and pain of that day, and there he was, sitting on one side of the fireplace, with Joan Plowright, his wife, opposite him. I will always love him for that moment. He insisted that we join him at their house in Brighton for the rest of that evening, which they turned from being a time of despair in to one of magic, communicating ideas about plays and acting far into the night, and relieving the grief of the stage-struck Foxes.

I think of Larry as the Invincible Laurence Olivier. I have marvelled at his work, along with the rest of the world. When I see him these days I am astounded at the courage that he shows in the face of ill health. It is incredible. One recent summer's day, I was sitting with him at a Sunday lunch party in his garden among a happy, informal group of friends. He was playing the perfect host, filling our glasses with champagne too often, keeping his audience spellbound with amusing stories, amazingly enough fresh ones about the theatre – always about the theatre.

Suddenly, he turned to his nurse, who was ever at his side. 'Take me upstairs, I want to go and rest,' he said, and in a second he became a very old, crumbling, infirm man, unable to walk without her support. As this pretty girl led him away, silence fell upon his guests, broken by a National Theatre actor. 'How awful to see Larry as ill as that.'

I hope I was not being unkind when I answered him, 'Of course he is not well, but if he was young and fit and suddenly decided he had done enough entertaining for the moment, he could have given that same performance, perfect in every detail.' I only said this because Larry had told me when I arrived that morning that he had just swum thirty lengths of his swimming pool. I had looked at his nurse. I had thought he was teasing. She had nodded. He was telling the truth.

And it was the same story when I went with my daughter-in-law, the actress Joanna David, who was staying with me, to dine with him at his house not very far from Buntings, my present cottage in Cuckfield.

This was in 1987, on the day after the fabulous and hugely publicized eightieth birthday celebration that had been arranged in his honour at the National Theatre, the monument he created. Cheered till the roof blew off the building by a standing audience comprised of all the great names of the entertainment business world-wide, who were shouting and clapping when he entered the box, he must have had to stand for a quarter of an hour, waving all over the house trying to thank us all. At one moment a huge birthday cake arrived on stage and out jumped his younger daughter, Julie-Kate, who flung her arms towards him, crying 'Happy Birthday, Daddy!' Peter Hall, dressed up as Shakespeare, hadn't the faintest idea what the Bard had prepared for him.

I went with Edward. We are two highly intolerant theatre-goers, so having applauded our fill we scurried away, only to run slap into John Mortimer. 'What did you think?' he asked. 'Wasn't the whole thing a disaster,' I said. It wasn't until I was outside that I realized he'd written much of it.

But Edward and I agreed that Olivier was already one of the immortals – Keane, Garrick, Irving, Tree, household names now. Perhaps he would be the greatest of them all.

Edward's wife, Joanna, came down to the country with me the following day. She is a very good friend of Joan Plowright, Larry's wife, and she had learned from her that Larry O, as I always call him, had done a bunk to his country hideout. He was alone with one of his young, ever-changing nurses, and Joan said she felt a visit from us would be appreciated.

Off we set. He lives, as the crow flies, a very short distance from my home, but to say his hideout is off the beaten track would be an understatement – not a habit I indulge in easily. In twenty minutes we turned off the main road and found ourselves in an uncultivated jungle. At one moment we had to use swap hooks to make a way for the car because it was pitch dark and I had driven off the dirt track that led to the house. We had been forewarned and so we were forearmed. It had rained a lot and our Wellington boots were soon full of slush. There was no need for bodyguards or alsatians – I think impenetrable jungles must shortly come back in fashion – because when we finally got through to the house and garden all was order, sweetness and light, and the lights from the house even showed what a large part Larry's covered swimming pool played in the garden.

He was waiting for us, his mood seemed quiet. He was alone with his nurse in this country house so far from anywhere. He had waited to open the champagne until we arrived, and as we walked in he did this. We raised our glasses, 'Many, many, many happy returns, darling Larry.'

'Oh yes, come to think of it I believe my birthday is around now.'

'Was yesterday, you mean. I hope you enjoyed it as much as we did. Even you, who are so used to fantastic receptions, must have been moved by that one . . .'

He turned and gave me a deadpan stare. He appeared not to have the faintest memory of the night before, or to have any idea what we were referring to. Only a doctor could possibly have told whether he was faking or whether he is living in the past and forgets immediately something as it happens to him. I remember feeling strange and rather disturbed and wanting to understand, hoping this would help him to enjoy an evening, just with Joanna and me, and that it would not seem too much of an anti-climax after the acclaim and tribute to a fantastic career that he had received just a few hours before.

We had a pleasant, very ordinary, dinner – stewed steak, I think – and he talked to me at length and in great and accurate detail about the past. It came vividly alive for him and for both of us, and then, with the same sudden decision that he had made at the lunch party, he announced like a child to his nanny: 'I want to go to bed', and his nurse led him upstairs like a child.

I do not know, nor ever shall, whether this great actor was using me or anyone who happened to be around as an audience for a performance.

Joanna and I had watched him disappear through a door on the arm of his young and pretty New Zealand nurse. She was most caring towards her patient, but will have known as much about him as we did of the far country from which she came, which was absolutely nothing. We had gathered from some amused remark of his that it was her admirer who was in the kitchen and who had cooked our dinner, and there was no doubt that once she had performed her professional duty impeccably she would do what was the most natural thing in the world, namely join her beloved.

Fumbling our way in the pitch darkness Joanna and I found our car, which then had to be manoeuvred over at least a mile of bends and bumps while we tried to avoid the over-hanging trees that were scraping our windscreen, until we finally got on to the main road, and I could put my foot on the accelerator and make for home. It was only then that we could speak of the friend we had left behind in his deserted hideout. I presumed that, like all actors, he kidded himself that he 'must get away from it all'. This is the fantasy of the actor who is lonely. In fact he longs for an audience, even a small one, to watch him play his scene.

As we cruised along the main road, Joanna said, 'Isn't Larry sweet? Do you think he is all right?'

I laughed. 'No, I don't think he is sweet. That is the one thing he is not.' I did not add that, of course, in my terms he was not all right at all. His aloneness was huge, like everything else about him.

My thoughts turned to Rex Harrison playing Captain Shotover in *Heartbreak House*, and how he, or Bernard Shaw – or the two of them together – had made the fact that the very young Ellie Dunn really loved the old man understandable to me as it had never been before. On the subject of Larry, I thought, I must be getting old to have a glimpse of what is meant by love and that this is all that matters. 'Sure,' I said, 'Larry is fine.' I just wished I meant it.

Driving home, I remembered something else Edward had told me about him. They had quite recently been making a film together in Berlin. Larry had been playing Rudolph Hess and after Edward had finished all he had to do and was ready for his return to England, he chose to remain in Berlin just to watch this extraordinary man play a short scene, which showed Hess coming out of prison for a brief moment and then wanting to go back immediately to the security of the world he knew. Freedom was not for him. Many 'takes' were necessary, but never for a moment did

Edward want to make for home. He stayed behind, moved and riveted by this amazing performer.

I saw Larry and Joan again later in 1987 at a Boxing Day party at the home of their agent, Laurence Evans, who had been my husband's partner. He gave me the usual affectionate hug and kiss. I asked him, 'How are you today, Larry?'

'Not at all bad, I have swum my thirty lengths.' On this occasion he went one better and was the life and soul of a huge, informal lunch party. All the guests had helped themselves to food and drink, and tables and chairs were scattered around the house, so we gathered in groups and sat about enjoying ourselves. I was sitting with Toby Rowland, an American producer, and his wife, Millie, and another producer, Australian this time, called Alan Davis. We were joined by Lady Richardson, the widow of Sir Ralph, and my son, Edward. We had found a table in the big kitchen and we were enjoying ourselves watching this collection of the most celebrated actors and actresses in England queueing up happily, taking their turn to be served lunch. The din of chatter and laughter was horrendous. It was a vast, happy and, for a moment, carefree party.

Suddenly, above the noise we heard singing. The kitchen fell quiet. It was carols. 'Carol singers must have come up from the village. Let's go and listen.' We moved to find them and got as far as the dining-room.

There sat Larry at the head of the long table with his two daughters and, nearest to him, my granddaughter, Emilia. He was singing with gusto at the top of his huge voice, leading this sophisticated choir and turning them all back into little children for a moment with 'Oh come all ye faithful, joyful and triumphant . . .' As I said to Laurence Evans, 'A line I had never expected to hear where that particular audience was gathered together!'

The room became packed. Soon all these famous figures from the world of the theatre were singing at the top of their lungs. But the Invincible Laurence Olivier was the focus, as he must always be, of all eyes and ears. He led this choir. He could lead any of us anywhere.

Epilogue

I started out stage struck and star struck, and, although I have sat in the gallery, in the upper circle, the stalls, and even in a box – on good days – ever since I was a child, my imagination was captured and has remained in captivity. I feel as excited today on entering a theatre as I ever did.

Life in the theatre for me started in the gallery. It was from this vantage point that one particular performance entranced me which has stayed in my mind, and there it will be as long as I am around. The venue was the Theatre Royal, Margate. The play was *The Scarlet Pimpernel*, the leading actors Fred Terry and his wife, Julia Nielson Terry. Any actor since then who has tried to play the elegant dandy, the SAS type hiding behind the aristocratic fop, falls short of Fred Terry. If you speak of this sort of acting today, it sounds old-fashioned, but I have a strong feeling that he would still pack them in. He was hypnotic, he enraptured his audience. He captured my heart then – he was the theatre, and I have been its prisoner ever since.

From the gallery at Margate I have worked my way down

towards the stage itself via the upper circle to the dress circle and so the stalls. Modern children who start their theatre-going in the stalls miss an awful lot. The real atmosphere, the glamour, the mystery, the excitement, are <u>in</u> the gallery. I sit in the stalls now as a matter of course, but the gilt is rather off the gingerbread.

I often feel very detached, not having the faintest idea what some of the modern playwrights are driving at and not even making much effort to find out, so my thoughts drift, as was the case recently when I was invited to our most important subsidized theatre to see a revival. As thrilled to be going to the theatre as I always have been, I arrived ten minutes ahead of my host and stood in the foyer, as there was nowhere to sit, watching the audience as they came in. A more depressing, ill-dressed, grubby, unkempt lot, all ready and willing to pay for very expensive seats, it is impossible to imagine. My spirits flagged. I admire my host very much, he is one of England's best set designers, so I had been to the hairdresser and gone home and changed. I felt out of it, old-fashioned and silly, and also very pleased that this was so.

My host arrived. 'Shall we go to our seats?'

'I'd love to. I have never seen this theatre, but I have heard so much about it.' In we went, took our seats. They must get the Queen's Award for discomfort, and never, but never, have I seen such a hideous auditorium.

Actors used to create an image, off-stage as well as on, that their public could enjoy. This was good for morale generally, both sides of the curtain. It took a great effort, and showed self-respect and pride in their calling. Now off-stage they look as drab as their audience, deny that they want to be stars, and say that the system is wrong. They do a great disservice to their profession. If they are holding a mirror up to nature, it is a very sad glass reflecting mediocrity. The denigration of the star system is due to laziness and refusal to try for the 1st XI in case they cannot make it, let alone sustain the effort and discipline required to stay there.

I mentioned this to a young, but extremely successful, actress who is the exception that proves the rule. She told me my intolerance showed a lack of understanding of the theatre of today. She pointed out that what we have now is a directors' theatre; they are the people who matter, they interpret the author's message for the audience and create an overall picture. It is their personality and their interpretation that counts . . . and they don't want stars. Alas, I see that what she said is true, but it is a phase that I trust will pass. Star quality in any walk of life is something that cannot be suppressed and in the theatre I could give a number of examples. For the moment I will just cite Maggie Smith.

*

When you are cast as the Grieving Widow, it is a very demanding and selfish role, and one most likely never to have been rehearsed. A very powerful director, who is called Mr I-Am-Fate, puts you upstage centre and says, 'Now get on with it.' The moment you are well into the part, getting the hang of it, he shouts, 'That's it, now we'll try someone else.' No one comes up and says, 'That's it for today, we'll telephone you,' and for some reason you cannot get to a stage-door or find the word Exit anywhere, you have to stay on a crowded stage and join a band of bewildered players, all wondering why they are there, and if the play will ever take shape and, if it does, will there be a part for you?

Well, perhaps there was never a part for me in the accepted sense of the term, but when I started to see through my tears of self-pity and frustration, I found a small corner where I could sit on my own and observe and try to write about the production, always hoping against hope that one day I might be called to play a part, even a walk-on.

Looking back, though, what a happy ending my life has been for a stage-struck girl. My childhood fantasy, that I would actually be friends with very famous people, especially in the theatre, has become a reality. A very poor ambition that may be, but it obsessed my younger self. I used to make up imaginary stories about all the well-known people I knew. What a sweet irony it is that many of them have become my very good friends, influencing my life and the lives of my children. These interesting people, life enhancers I suppose I could call them, have come from so many different walks of life, not just from the world of the theatre. Perhaps the most gratifying thing has been that some of these men and women I have so admired have liked me enough to be severe with me quite often and take me to task when they saw I was behaving foolishly. Without dimming the stars in my eyes they have helped me to see where I have sometimes gone wrong. They have helped me to know myself and better still to forget myself, by showing me a bigger picture of what it's all about.

To give just one example, Robert Morley helped me again, though he cannot have known it. I recalled standing in a street with him in Le Touquet. We had just left an afternoon session at the Casino and we started to argue about a child who was ill and not being well handled or sympathetically understood.

'But Robert, this is awful. What will happen to this child? It's so unhappy, how will it survive?'

'Don't be so patronizing. Why shouldn't any child, all children, if you like, do as well or even better than you have?'

His voice from the past helped me yet again to brace up and dismiss self-pity and get on with my own life, so I sharpened my pencil and got ready to write about something we all have to do, which is to come to terms with ourselves. I thought I would write, and confess as I tell the story, about how often I have been Completely Foxed.

Index

Farce About Face

Brian Rix

All who have ever laughed at Brian Rix's theatrical performances, warmed to his genial nature during TV and radio interviews, or been moved to admiration by his involvement with MENCAP will find his latest 'touch of the memoirs' absorbing reading.

Sequel to the bestselling *My Farce From My Elbow*, the hilariously anecdotal *Farce About Face* shines the spotlight on a life packed with incident, on the giddy world of show business, on an abiding enthusiasm for cricket and a passionate private and public commitment to people with a mental handicap.

By turns comic and moving, Sir Brian charts the achievements of a career that has come full circle to encompass a theatrical second coming in the classic farce *Dry Rot*, thrilling once again his legions of loyal fans.

'A proud story.' *Sunday Telegraph*

'Fascinating.' *Birmingham Post*

'A doughty fighter, and a refreshing book.' *Daily Express*

FONTANA PAPERBACKS

Fontana Paperbacks
Non-fiction

Fontana is a leading paperback publisher of non-fiction. Below are some recent titles.

- ☐ McCartney: The Biography *Chet Flippo* £4.50
- ☐ Shirley Temple: American Princess *Anne Edwards* £4.50
- ☐ The Salad Days *Douglas Fairbanks Jr* £4.95
- ☐ Jane Fonda *Michael Freedland* £3.95
- ☐ Oh I Say! *Dan Maskell* £4.50
- ☐ The Thirties and After *Stephen Spender* £2.50
- ☐ If Voting Changed Anything, They'd Abolish It
      Ken Livingstone £3.95
- ☐ The Boys and the Butterflies *James Birdsall* £2.95

You can buy Fontana paperbacks at your local bookshop or newsagent. Or you can order them from Fontana Paperbacks, Cash Sales Department, Box 29, Douglas, Isle of Man. Please send a cheque, postal or money order (not currency) worth the purchase price plus 22p per book for postage (maximum postage required is £3).

NAME (Block letters) _____

ADDRESS _____

_____

_____